GU01019175

SOMETHING
OF MY
LIFE

Whose I am, and Whom I serve.

Acts 27:23

James G. Hutchinson

Distributed by:
Ards Evangelical Book Shop
7 High Street, Newtownards, Co Down,
N Ireland, BT23 4JN

November, 1997
Published by:
Gospel Tract Publications
85 Portman Street, Glasgow G41 1EJ

ISBN 0 948417 79 X
Copyright © 1997
James G. Hutchinson

Typeset and printed by
Gospel Tract Publications
Glasgow, Scotland.

APPRECIATION

I am indebted to Mr J W Ferguson for his help in checking the material and making useful suggestions.
Also to Mr J G Wilson for doing all the typing.

James G Hutchinson

Contents

Foreword

Imagine my surprise when I was asked to write a *Foreword* for this book, as there are many others who are much more capable, however, as I've known the author since we were in our late teens or early twenties, I consider it an honour to do so.

Our fathers were evangelists here in Northern Ireland, so we were raised in homes where preachers were regular visitors and gospel meetings were the main topic of conversation. Consequently as young believers we, too, in the goodness of God became interested in spreading the gospel and were encouraged by older brethren and often taken to share in gospel meetings. In those days we were both shop assistants, so we've had quite a lot in common.

As J G H helped in the gospel he became convinced that God was calling him to full time service. The intervening years, I feel sure, have proved beyond all doubt that it "pleased God to call him by His grace...that he might preach..." (Galatians 1:15-16). I believe like Saul of Tarsus he was a chosen vessel, gifted to preach the gospel with simplicity, sincerity and dignity. My father often said when he heard Mr Hutchinson preach the gospel that he felt "there's a man at his right job!" Many have thanked God that Mr Hutchinson came their way with the gospel and that God used his preaching to lead them to concern and to the Saviour.

I have no doubt that with his friendly disposition and business acumen he would have done really well in business, but the Bible says, "He that winneth souls is wise", and I have often felt that, "he hath chosen that good part", Luke 10:42. Mr Hutchinson is a real soul winner with a great interest in the families of the believers.

I recall that during holidays in our early days we helped in Open Air Meetings on the Town Hall Green at Portrush nightly at 10.00 p m when crowds filled the streets and many listened to the gospel. We shared a series of gospel meeetings in Antrim a few years ago and God was pleased to bless and save a few souls, and what a joy it was to labour with him.

I've followed Mr Hutchinson's labours over the years with

interest. He has kept a steady course and like Mordecai has been "accepted of the multitude of his brethren", Esther 10:3.

J G H has often stayed in our home and we have enjoyed his fellowship. During these years (well over 50) we have had a happy and unmarred friendship and I am happy to consider him one of my closest friends — a friend whose confidence and counsel I appreciate.

I trust that many will enjoy reading of his labours in the gospel and that many will be challenged as to their own lives and cry out like Saul of Tarsus — "Lord what wilt Thou have me to do" — find out and do it.

I'm sure we all hope Mr Hutchinson will be long spared to continue his gospel preaching and helpful ministry to the believers with the Lord's blessing.

J S Wallace
Sept 1997

Family Background and Conversion

I was born in Carryduff, County Down, on 13th September 1920, the second of a family of four, one girl and three boys. I was given the name of my two grandparents, James for James Spence, my mothers father, and Greer for my father's father, W Greer Hutchinson. My parents both came from the Carryduff area. My mother's father was a prosperous farmer. My father's father was principal of the local school. Both my grandparents were God-fearing Presbyterians. My father was encouraged to be active in the local church, teaching the Bible class and leading the choir. In that day there was no musical instrument in the church, so with his tuning fork and true tenor voice he led the praise. Despite all this, and an honourable life, he was a stranger to God's salvation, a devout, honest young man, but not on the way to Heaven. He would have said that often from early boyhood days, when he would be reminded of the Saviour and His suffering and death, strange feelings of interest and emotion came to him.

His first real awakening to eternal matters came on one summer evening when, after the church service, he was standing at the gate of his home, and heard singing and then the distinct voice of a local farmer, Mr T Maxwell, quoting the words of Ecclesiastes 11:9 "Rejoice, O young man, in thy youth, and let thy heart cheer thee in the days of thy youth, and walk in the ways of thine heart, and in the sight of thine eyes: but know thou, that for all these things God will bring thee into judgment." Carryduff was then only a very small village and the folk who conducted the meeting were few in number. Little did they know how God would use His word that evening and the blessing that would flow out to others in many places

From that evening he had deep soul trouble and tried all he could think of to have peace with God, but seemingly with no success. On one occasion, in despair, he decided to give it all up and made his way to a theatre in the city. Just as the curtain went up imitation tongues of fire were shown and immediately a voice seemed to say, "If you are not saved you will be in a far worse fire," He left the place at once to walk home to Carryduff, a sinner in deep despair.

Hearing of an outstanding evangelist conducting meetings in a large public building in the city, he thought he would go there. The large company and the good singing appealed to him, as did the evangelist's straightforward preaching. As he left the building a kind gentleman, no doubt discerning his unhappy appearance, said, 'Young man are you saved?' When he replied that he was not, but would like to be, his friend said, 'Wait and we will speak with you.' After some prayer and scripture reading, he was asked to read a verse. When he did, he was asked, 'Do you believe that?' He said, 'Of course I do.' 'Well then,' said the man, 'you are saved,' and produced a card to be signed. It was only a matter of a short time until he knew all was not well as he had no peace or the sense of sins forgiven.

That experience left lasting impressions and while he realised that many in such circles were sincere, and at times God worked and blessing was given, he saw the danger of methods which might make people think they were saved when they were not. Peace and salvation came to him while he was at his employment. Leaving the others, he closed himself in a little cloakroom and cried to God for mercy. Apart from human agency, God can save, and in that little room God used the words of 1 John 1:7 to bring peace and assurance of salvation: "The blood of Jesus Christ His Sin cleanseth us from all sin."

Shortly after that, feeling his own unworthiness and the fact of indwelling sin, he became greatly distressed. He went to a meeting to hear Mr David Rea. Two things were emphasised that helped him, and he would have said remained with him all his life. Psalm 116:1 "I love the Lord" was dealt with. His heart responded at once and said, 'That is true of me.' Later in his message Mr Rea drew attention to Colossians 2:8, "Ye are complete in Him," causing him to see that his acceptance was not in any way due to his merit or attainment, but was all in Christ. His interest in divine matters grew and developed and he began to be aware of God's pathway for His children. It became clear to him that he should be baptised and be where he could, in simplicity, carry out the desire of the Lord Jesus, when in the upper room He said to His own, "This do in remembrance of me."

Conveying these desires to his parents created quite a stir. His father, who was the senior elder in the church, felt he was making a great mistake in leaving where he had been brought up and was so active and useful, and did everything he could to dissuade him. He offered to put him through for the Presbyterian ministry, or if he wished he would set him up in business. He put it to him plainly: "I'll do anything I can for you, but if you persist in what you speak of you must leave the home and take your belongings with you." While he valued home and family, such was his conviction regarding the truth of God, that at this crisis point, and while the cost was high and caused many a lonely night and silent tears, he never once regretted obeying the Lord, and God honoured and blessed him for it. The words of the Psalm were of great comfort and help to him. "When my father and mother forsake me, then the Lord will take me up." Psalm 27:10. He dearly loved his family and had the joy later, not only to see them coming to his meetings, but rejoicing in salvation.

Where I was brought up, Bannview Cottage, Banbridge.

He was baptised and received into Apsley Street assembly, Belfast. Later, after marriage, residing in the area, he was in fellowship in the Lessans assembly, from which he was commended to the work of the Lord in 1917.

My mother, Miss Sarah Spence, was saved at meetings in Carryduff in 1914. Mr J Stewart and Mr H Bailie had the meetings in a vacant house and God gave them a season of blessing, when my mother, and others of the family were added to Lessans assembly.

In 1921, as a family, we went to live in Banbridge. My parents were very happy in the assembly and the Christians were kind to us as children. Our home was about a mile from the town and each Lord's day after the breaking of bread to which we were always taken, with a short time before Sunday School, we had our dinner in various homes. I often think of the care and kindness of those dear believers, not to mention the patience they needed to care for mischievous children! Though it is well over seventy years ago, I clearly remember some of the first lessons I was taught, things that gave me to know my condition and need, and principles taught regarding manner of life and general behaviour.

From my earliest days I had serious thoughts about eternal matters and being right with God. When in the home the family gathered around to sing. Often the singing of the old hymn 'When mother's of Salem' stirred me and I used to think, 'If He was here now I would come to Him.' On one occasion, when I was staying with my grandmother and aunt on the farm at Killynure, a Mr Edward Hughes, a converted Roman Catholic, was staying in the home, while having gospel meetings in the Lessans assembly hall. While only a young fellow I would have loved to be saved. Standing at the farm gate I thought, 'If I believed enough, and in the right way, then something would come over me and I would know I was saved,' but it does not work that way!

Often when walking to School I was approached by an aged Baptist pastor and spoken to about my salvation. I am deeply thankful for all who prayed for me and took an interest in my welfare and only eternity will reveal how much I owe to the prayerful intercession of God's dear people. It was in September 1934 that I got saved. Mr W Johnston and my father commenced

Father, Mother and self.

gospel meetings in a tent erected at Huntly, on the outskirts of Banbridge, and when listening to the preaching and hearing of others getting saved, I became concerned. This seemed to come to a crisis when one night one of those preachers spoke on the solemn words of Isaiah 14:9, "Hell from beneath is moved for thee to meet thee at thy coming." The two words, "for thee", seemed to reach me in power. I literally trembled on the seat, but I did more. I made up my mind, 'If there is salvation for Jim Hutchinson, I will have it in these meetings.' A few nights after that God in His mercy saved me while quietly sitting listening to the preaching. As one speaker was closing his message he quoted the words of Matthew 11:28, "Come unto Me all ye that labour and are heavy laden, and I will give you rest." It came to me like this: "Who is the speaker?" I was clear and happy about this, "He is the one who died for me." What is the saying? "Come unto Me." I wasn't occupied with my coming, I was occupied with the blessed one Who died for me, and while it may not have been the language of my lips, it was the response of my weary, sin-burdened heart: "O Lamb of God I come".

I thought as I left the tent, "I will not say anything to anyone, but I will see how it will be in a day or two." However, as I cycled through the town a Christian farmer said to me, "Jim, do you ever think of being saved?" Almost before I realised, I said, "I got saved in the meeting tonight!" How the news got home before me I don't know, but it did, and God was thanked by my parents and the many who prayed for me. The next day at school I told a young man who sat at the desk beside me—a nice young man from a good family, who later in life became a clergyman. He thought I was out of my mind!

Assembly Life in Banbridge

Leaving school, which my parents did not altogether like, I was given a job in a local retail shoe business, where I was particularly happy. I still like shoes! It would be the first thing I would notice on a man, woman or child! I was a short time there when I was put in charge of the gents department where I continued until I was 21.

One of the overseeing brethren approached me regarding baptism and assembly fellowship. I believe this to be a wise thing to do — not to push anyone beyond their exercise, but to keep a watchful eye, and where there are signs of life, give encouragement. I was soon baptised and received into the assembly at Banbridge. The same beloved elder said to me, "Jim, when I was young I kept very quiet in the assembly. I regret that now, don't you do it!" The first few years of my Christian life were more or less on the normal level of young believers. I attended all the meetings and companied with several young men of my own age. With other young men I gave out tracts, went to open-air meetings and wherever there was assembly activity, we were encouraged to be there.

One of the young men with whom I companied, a little older than I was and better off, bought a car, a Ford Eight for £98 on the road, and petrol was cheap. On Sunday evenings we went here and there to preach at the evening meetings. On one particular occasion, I took for my subject 'The Day of Atonement!' I question if I would do it now. An older sister as she shook hands with me at the door said, "If you live, you might be a preacher yet." However I could never make up my mind whether she was serious or sarcastic.

A crisis in my spiritual experience came when Mr David Craig was having meetings in Banbridge hall. One Lord's Day afternoon he linked Leviticus chapter 1, the 'voluntary offering', with Romans 12:1 'present your bodies a living sacrifice'. God helped His servant and the message reached my heart, and although the hall was full, I felt as if I was the only one

J G Hutchinson, 21 years.

The girl I left home for; Elsie J Martin

in the place. The meeting closed with the words, "What glad return can I impart for favours so divine? O take my all, my weary heart and make it only Thine." While I have not been able to attain to it as I would have liked, life was different from that day. I realised I was not my own, and I willingly gave my all to the One Who has shed His blood to make me His. That experience was as real as my conversion.

Just a little diversion: Mr Craig gave us a number of messages on coming events. This was in 1939, He was quite clear that Hitler and the Italian leader could not possibly form an axis. The meetings were hardly over until they did. Mr McCabe, who was very fond of David, said jokingly, "He had good meetings but he put himself among the minor prophets".

Londonderry — Happy Days

In 1941 when I was approached and offered a situation as manager of a shoe store in Londonderry City, I felt I should accept and go. I had never stayed away from home, and had no knowledge of Londonderry. The Sunday evening before I left a brother opening the Gospel meeting gave out an unusual hymn for a gospel meeting, but lines in it were to me like sweet music from heaven, a real blessing to me that night, and many times since:

Through this changing world below
Lead me gently, gently as I go.
Trusting Thee I cannot stray,
I can never, never lose my way

An elderly sister in the assembly gave me a pair of gold cuff links with a verse of scripture on a small piece of paper, a verse which in a sense fully described her and was to be a voice to me, 'Not slothful in business, fervent in spirit, serving the Lord', Romans 12:1. I still treasure and sometimes use the cuff links. In mid August 1941, with my case and my letter of commendation, I arrived in Londonderry. Lodgings had been arranged for me with two sisters from the assembly, who said I could stay for a month until I got my bearings. This month extended to three and a half years and I was happy there and well cared for in every way. Often visiting speakers would stay there also, and it was my privilege to meet many of the Lord's servants, and to receive from them guidance and encouragement.

I was warmly welcomed to the assembly, which at that time had 120 in fellowship, with three Sunday Schools, a well attended Sunday evening gospel meeting, and a large annual conference. The assembly was active with men and women in it who were spiritual, praying people — a delightful atmosphere for a young man away from home and friends. I thank God for those happy days where I was encouraged to help in the Sunday School and in open-air work. Those were the dark days of the second world war. Londonderry was an important naval base on the western approaches, and the city was alive with naval, airforce and USA technicians. Many of these were contacted and given tracts and encouraged to come into the meetings. In the East Wall Gospel Hall there was quite a large basement, which some thought would be a good place to have a late Sunday evening meeting specially for the sailors, soldiers etc. It was called the 'Forces Meeting'. Cards were printed and quite a number went out onto the streets to try and get these dear men in to a session of bright, happy singing when someone would give their testimony, and another have a short simple gospel message. Then refreshments would be served, and at times there would be quite a time of conversation and discussion on spiritual matters. Some introduced an organ to help with the singing (I doubt if it ever does). A brother said, "They brought in a new cart and it must have had rubber wheels — we didn't hear it coming".

We met several believers from various parts and the local Christians opened their homes to them, but we were very sad when we would walk down with the sailors to the ships and bid them good-night. Several of these ships were sunk and the crews lost. Some dear believers went home to Heaven from the cold waters of the Atlantic Ocean. Many others who received tracts and heard the gospel, only God knows where they are. Such thoughts make us wonder if we did enough in reaching out with the gospel. Did we seize the opportunities as we should have?

I found a change in the Londonderry assembly from that in Banbridge. I came into the assembly because I knew it was where God would have me be, but strictly speaking, I had not much conviction. In Banbridge, we were all of one mind, and the assembly meetings occupied our time and attention. While there were evangelistic groups in the town, we knew them and were on good terms, yet there never seemed to be the slightest suggestion of associating with them in their activities. In Londonderry I discovered there were spiritual people whose outlook was different. They felt they could happily attend and take part in the meetings of the various groups. Some of them were large, and attendance at their gospel meetings was good, and God gave blessing.

In some way I thank God I was faced with such a situation. It caused me to look carefully into the Scriptures and discover for myself exactly what the mind of God was. After a good deal of study and prayerful exercise I came to this conclusion that all I could find in the New Testament was the assembly, and if it was of God, I believed then and still do, that all I had to offer would go to the building up of what God had made provision for.

Why should I, either by my presence or preaching, support that for which there was no scriptural foundation? While I came to this decision, I did not become unfriendly with these dear folk. I see no justification for unkind words or actions as one notices from time to time — the Scriptures speak of "the truth in love". In the midst of differing opinions, Paul said to the Galatian saints, "The fruit of the Spirit is love, joy, peace, long-suffering, gentleness, goodness, faith, meekness, temperance". All who engage in the work of the Lord, and seek to "hold fast the form of sound words" should give careful thought to such words.

One of the gentlemen, active and capable in gospel and ministry in one of these groups who was in conversation with me (many a friendly verbal battle we had) said to me, "I suppose you think that company of people with whom you meet is perfect". He hardly expected the reply. I said, "How could it be when a brother like you with such ability and a good testimony is not in it?" How good and useful would companies of Christians be if, like those in Acts 2:44, they were "all together in one place". I often think the coming of the Lord will do two things. It will unite all true believers "caught up together". It will separate them from all that is not of God. Another incident with that same brother comes to mind. One day he approached me and asked if I would speak at one of the gospel meetings he was responsible for. I felt I would need to make the position clear. I said "If I go and should feel free that God would have me read the story of the Ethiopian eunuch, I would have to read all the story, and see how and when the man was baptised. Would your people like that?" He hesitated for a moment, then said, "I don't think they would." My reply was simple and direct, "I wouldn't be happy to go where I could not take all the Word of God with me." We parted the best of friends, and were that until he died.

As I became increasingly engaged in cottage meetings and in a

variety of places, some of them in the city and districts around,
the conviction was growing that God would have me give my
life to the gospel. On several occasions I was asked by the elders
if I had thought of this, but being unsure, I was non-commital.

Business was doing well, and we had moved to much larger
premises. My employer was good to me and I was very happy
with a nice staff. I was also happily married. This took place in
1944. My bride came from Banbridge, Miss Elsie J Martin. She
was saved as a teenager at meetings Mr Stewart and Mr
Bingham had and was in fellowship in the assembly. Mr
Bingham performed the wedding ceremony on 11th April 1944.
This, of course, meant I left my lodgings, and we secured a place
to live in the city. A brother I know said he did two good things
in life. Mentioning his wife's name, he said, "I got saved and I got
married" — I could well say the same! God gave us two girls,
who throughout the years have brought us much joy. Both
were saved in early life. Early in christian life they manifested
interest in divine matters and we are thankful that their interest
continues. The younger girl, living in England, has no family.
The other, living in Northern Ireland, has two children, a boy
and a girl. Both are in assembly fellowship along with their
husbands and are active in the work of God. The debt that I, and
my girls, owe to their mother could not be expressed in words.
Her constant care and prayerful advice, her christian conduct in
the home and at all times, has been to the family a living example
of christian motherhood.

Mr Robert Peacock had stepped out in full time gospel work.
He was to be joined in Letterkenny with Mr T H Lyttle. Mr
Lyttle was detained elsewhere and the brethren asked me if I
would give some help.

After business each evening I went over to Letterkenny by
bus and after the meeting spent the night in the home of Mr
Hadden McKinney and his mother. They were kind and good
friends to me as long as they lived. Each morning after breakfast
was made by candlelight (these were the days of blackout) I
would get the Lough Swilly train and be in time to open up the
shop. Mr Peacock continued for some years in those border
areas. He was a good visitor and a good simple gospel preacher. I
joined him again, first in a portable hall at Carrigans, Co
Donegal, where there was a nice interest and some blessing in

Wedding 1944.

salvation. He was living in the portable hall and I stayed there after the meeting each night at his invitation. He was a good cook, and sometimes I think I can still smell the bacon as he made the breakfast. Carrigans being only a few miles from Londonderry I cycled to and fro. Leaving Carrigans after some weeks we moved over to St Johnston and were able to have meetings in the Orange hall. They were well attended, but I thought not so good as at Carrigans. As far as we could gather the only other assembly meetings conducted there was when Mr James Clark was there something like 35-40 years earlier. Mr Sam Lewis spent many years labouring in County Donegal and neighbouring counties. He and Mr Peacock and I tried meetings in Ture between Londonderry and Moville but we found little interest. Around the same time we had some meetings in a farmhouse where the owner was saved, but his wife and son were not. We were happy to see them and a few neighbours under the sound of the gospel each night. Some weeks later, a local brother, Mr McClements and I got the use of a hall belonging to the B Specials. We were a very short time there when we were told we could no longer have the use of the hall. When we made discreet enquiries we learned that a preacher in a large neighbouring congregation was responsible for the situation. But it is wonderful how on occasions Satan's purposes can be overruled. A short distance from where we were there was an old barn on an out-farm belonging to a brother in the Londonderry assembly. He said we would be very welcome to use it but it needed a good deal of fixing up. This was attended to and the meetings went ahead. A nice young woman got saved who later became a devoted Sunday School teacher. But more, such was the interest it was thought to commence a Sunday School which was carried on for years by the local Christians.

If we had been allowed the continued use of the B Specials hall likely a few weeks would have seen it all over, but God saw to it that the work continued for years at Ballymagroarty. On the outskirts of the Waterside area of Londonderry there was a little hall owned by some Christians. When Mr McClements, who lived nearby, asked if we could use it he was assured we could without reservation of any kind. We had a happy fruitful series with nice numbers and some getting saved. On my first visit to

Maureen, Left; Margaret, Right.

the USA in 1956, just as I was opening my first ministry meeting, a young man and his wife walked in. It stirred me as he was one of those saved in the meetings at Kilfennan in the Waterside.

It was becoming increasingly clear to me that my future lay not in business, but in the work of the Lord, but where I was not sure. I thought of various parts of the world, and some missionaries visiting Londonderry showed an interest in me and spoke encouragingly of their field of labour. One dear man came specially to see me and as I look back at it he almost pressed me too much. I would have liked to accompany him as he returned to his place of labour where he was used and blessed of God, but I had no light. I talked to my father about it. He spent 45 years preaching in the UK. He was very happy in knowing about my exercise and encouraged me, but said, "It might be wise to try another field rather than the North of Ireland." Given that and the view of missionaries, I had deep exercise as to what to do. Each time I prayed about it the verse came in power (Matthew 2:13), the word of the Lord to Joseph, "be thou there until I bring thee word". I became convinced that God would have me stay in my own island home, and now after 50 years I have no doubt it was God's mind for me.

Stepping out in Full-time Service

I asked for a meeting with the oversight of the assembly to tell them of my exercise. I feel it is most important to consult men of spiritual standing and have their commendation. I would not have felt free to act without it

After the meeting was opened in prayer they asked me to tell of my exercise. When I did, I said to them, "I will now leave and you can discuss it and let me know". As I spoke the oldest member of the oversight and perhaps the best taught said, "Sit where you are. As far as we are concerned, the thing proceedeth from the Lord. We cannot speak unto thee bad or good" (Genesis 25:50). I was very happy and thankful to have their wholehearted commendation and I treasure the letter they gave me. All these dear men are now at home with the Lord. My next step was to see my employer. I went up to head office, but when I arrived my courage almost failed. I slipped quietly into a little cloakroom and pulled out a testament my mother had given me before I left Banbridge. I just let it fall open and the first words that caught my eye were Acts 16:10, "assuredly gathering that the Lord has called us for to preach the gospel." I went out to the office and told him what my intentions were. "Well," said he, "there is not much future in that life, you have a good job, and prospects are good." I replied, "Sir, you and I look at things from different angles." He said, "Yes I know that, but if you change your mind and come back, your job is there for you." I thanked him and felt relieved. He asked me if I would stay until they got a man to fill my place and this they did in about four weeks time. I will not soon forget 25th August 1946. The new manager came and I introduced him to the staff and things in general. I will admit as I gave him the keys and walked out I was not in a very buoyant frame of mind. No job, no money and my wife expecting our first child in November.

I went to my room to pray and as I did, the word of the Lord to Abraham (Genesis 15:1), I am thy shield and thy exceeding great reward", came in freshness and power, and how I can testify to God's faithfulness in keeping His promise. About midday the postman brought me a letter with five single pound notes and a line or two to say "a little token of fellowship with you in your new job". And five pounds was a fair bit of money in 1946.

Mr Lewis and I tried a few meetings at Culmore but with no success. Certainly not a very bright start for a preaching career! But brighter days were ahead. The assembly at Aughavey contacted me about joining Mr S Abernethy with them in gospel meetings. Mr Abernethy originally came from that district and, having sold his business in Dungannon, had concern about his old neighbours and their families.

I had not known Mr Abernethy before this but I did know his brother Willie, who often came to Londonderry with Mr W Rodgers to share the gospel meeting. In passing let me say this: no one was more helpful and encouraging to me when I went out preaching than Mr Rodgers. I value my many contacts with him and his counsel.

I found Mr Abernethy to be a Christian gentleman and soon discovered that this is what the people of the district thought of him. I didn't always agree with his views, which we discussed in an amicable way. One night after the meeting, and supper being over, we started to talk. I cannot honestly think of what the subject was, but I differed with him. Looking across the room at me he said, "You are tight", meaning I was conservative in my thoughts and ways. Mr T McVey with whom we were staying spoke and said, "Mr Abernethy, he cannot be, if he was he wouldn't be preaching with you or staying with me". I will long remember with thanksgiving Mr McVey's godly life and spiritual interest. He was given to worrying and sometimes wondered if he was saved. On one such occasion a hymn of Fanny Crosby's came to him, the opening words of which were "Saviour more than life to me". In the quietness of his own room he said, "That is true of me, the Saviour is more precious to me than life itself". "Sweetest comfort of my soul" — love to Christ is the touchstone.

We continued the meetings from November 1946 until February 1947. Not having a car and being quite a distance from home, we didn't get home at the weekends, so we thought, why not preach on Saturdays as well? This we did. It pleased God to create interest and several professed to be saved.

A retired, very religious man who attended the meetings got saved. He was quick to say to some of his relations, "I'm saved and I know it, but I'll not join the brethren", so we quietly left him alone. A short time after our meetings closed, on coming home from his church service, he said to his family, "There is something strange about it all. There he is with only one sermon and two short prayers and he read it all. The two men in the hall preached every night for weeks and never read a word of it, and I'll never be back." The divine life God gave him found nothing to which it could respond. Very soon he was baptised and received into the assembly, where he continued steadfastly for years until the Lord took him home.

After I finished in Aughavey I joined my father in Strabane. He was three weeks or so into the meetings at that stage and a nice interest had been seen, and some had alreay professed to be saved. My father was just recovering from a severe heart attack and was unable to be present in the closing nights.

Mr Rodgers and Mr Fairfield had had meetings in Strabane the previous year, and while they had excellent attendance, no one professed salvation. Writing to Mr Fairfield after he returned to Venezuela Mr Rodgers said, "John Hutchinson and his son are reaping where we sowed."

While we were in Strabane each Lord's Day afternoon we had a gospel meeting in Ardstraw. The assembly there was small, but with a gospel spirit they were able to get some neighbours in. Newtownstewart, some miles from Strabane, had several Christians living in the area who were in fellowship in Ardstraw assembly. They decided to have a breaking of bread meeting, which they did, in full fellowship with Ardstraw. It meant that both companies were small, but God has blessed in both places and they carry on maintaining a good gospel testimony. The Newtownstewart company asked my father for some gospel meetings, possibly thinking that the interest and blessing in Strabane would continue. We have all learned this is not always so, and my father would only stay a week. He felt there was not sufficient interest to stay for. I must admit, I would have liked to continue, but being young and inexperienced, I was happy to accept his decision.

Having acquired a new tent, through the kindness and generosity of the Lord's people, it was decided we should erect it in the Waterside area of Londonderry. We had a fruitful, happy summer, half of it in Waterside, half on the city side. Quite a number professed salvation, some who are now prominent in assembly life in other countries. A number of these, with others who had been saved earlier, were added to the assembly. During the last week of the meetings we had some nights of ministry, a night on baptism stands out in my mind. A nurse who had been saved for some time and very devoted to her place of worship attended. At the close of the meeting, she came to the platform, with her finger in the Bible at the place we had been reading from and quite firmly said, "If you are right, I am wrong, but I am right," We just left her with the Scriptures and soon after she requested baptism and assembly fellowship. For many years she has been a hard working missionary in a dark and needy land.

At the end of that summer I got a short note written on business paper, which read, "We, in Scrabo, are exercised about meetings in October, could you come? Yours faithfully, FC Glasgow. PS If you don't know who we are your father will tell you. FCG." I felt it was the mind of God for me to go, and this I arranged. When I arrived on a Saturday evening at Mr Glasgow's home where I was to stay, he greeted me at the door, brought me in and introduced me to his wife and daughter, then said, "I'll show you your room." His manner was brusque, and I wondered to myself as I unpacked my case, is this his usual or has something upset him. I had visited Mr James Megaw, evangelist, some days earlier as he was ill and getting towards the close of his life. When I told him where I was going for the meetings he said, "You will find Fred Glasgow all right," but after my first introduction, I wasn't so sure. However I soon found out he was correct in what he said, I found Mr Glasgow to be a successful business man, a keen student of the Scriptures and a man of christian integrity. But it took a little while! For the first three meetings, he sat like a stoic, looking at me over his half glasses. In one of the opening nights, I said, "You will remember that Scripture says." At supper he said, "You needn't ask these people if they remember, they don't know." Again I wondered if Mr Megaw was right. About the fourth night the hall was well filled and there was a measure of help. That night at supper he said with a smile, "That will do." I had passed! For twelve weeks I stayed and was kindly cared for by his gracious wife and daughter. Until his death he was a good friend and when he was taken home, I felt something had gone out of the district that has never been replaced. The assembly then meeting in the old hall up in the country arranged a 'memorial gospel' meeting and asked that I should speak. I based my message on Genesis 25:8-9. It was so nice to see Mr Glasgow's five sons present and all in assembly fellowship.

After about six weeks I thought we should close the meetings and when I mentioned this to the brethren they said, "We will agree with what you decide." So, on the Lord's day I announced that the meetings would finish on Wednesday night. After the meeting a young man in the assembly came to me and said, "You are wrong, the meetings should continue." I told him what the responsible brethren said, but he wasn't satisfied. So insistent was he that I announced we would have a few more nights. On the Thursday night the little hall was packed and an unsaved man and his wife could only get a seat one on either side of the aisle. As the meeting went on they both got saved and it was delightful to see them at the porch telling each other of being saved. The meetings continued another six weeks. I was nearly out of sermons!

In January of 1948, my father asked me to accompany him to Ahoghill for gospel meetings which I greatly enjoyed. It was my first visit to County Antrim. A good measure of the influence of the '59 revival' was apparent and the people were interested in divine matters and quite a sense of the 'fear and reverence of God' continued. The assembly testimony was good and the village folk attended well. One day when I was visiting from door to door inviting the people, a lady said to me, "Is that Bob's hall?" I said, "Yes, that's where he goes." "Well," said she, "If it is I'll go, for if there is a man in this district going to Heaven, it's Bob McMeekin." What an influence a consistent christian testimony has. God was gracious to us and several got saved. After Ahoghill we had a few meetings in the old hall at Rasharkin, but there was little interest and the meetings were not prolonged.

Years of Evangelism

For many years the Scottish assemblies carried on a good gospel work in tents during the summer season, and in 1948 my father and I were asked to be responsible for the tent work in Lanarkshire. My father had been to Coatbridge and adjoining areas and had seen blessing in salvation but I was an unknown quantity.

A medical doctor who originally came from Scotland and was living in Belfast said to me when he heard that I was going, "It will be good for you, for I know they can be critical hearers. It will help to make you careful." I soon learned that what he said was true, but I would have to say that they were all very helpful to me. At the opening conference I commenced by saying, "Deal gently with the young man" (1 Samuel 18:5). This they did and we had a very happy summer season. Our first pitch was at Stonehouse. Mr W Trew, Cardiff, himself a Scot said, "You will likely have good meetings at Calderbank, Stonehouse might be different." The order was reversed. We had excellent meetings in Stonehouse, a number got saved and some backsliders restored, and while numbers in Calderbank were quite good and we saw a little blessing in conversions, there was not the same movement we had seen in Stonehouse.

About mid summer I had a letter from Mr C McEwen, my first, asking if I would join him in a tent effort in Exeter for the month of September 1948. My father was going elsewhere and I was free, so I agreed, thus forming a friendship which remained unbroken until his death in 1992. I found him to be a man of strict integrity and sterling worth, who laboured diligently in Devon and Cornwall, and sought the upbuilding of the assemblies. The tent, seating around 600, was pitched in the Buller Road area of the city. The assemblies in the area rallied around and heartily supported the meetings. Mr McEwen was a simple straightforward preacher, and as I was of the same thought, we seemed to suit each other and the saints responded. We had large meetings with several professing to be saved. Such

Lanarkshire Tent, Stonehouse, 1948.

was the interest the Christians thought we should try another effort, suggesting September 1950, to which we consented in the will of God. This time the tent was larger and we had greater numbers, but not the same blessing.

As soon as I came home from Exeter I started in Comber, a Unitarian town. The assembly was heartily united and anxious to see the hand of God at work. I greatly enjoyed day-to-day visiting in the town, and with one or two exceptions was well received. Not being far from Scrabo and Newtownards we had a good measure of support from both assemblies. I have noticed in recent years that assemblies do not support each other's gospel efforts as once they did. Various reasons may be given, but I wonder is it not a sign of less concern for the perishing.

The work of the local Christians, coupled with help from other assemblies and constant daily visitation helped to fill the hall each night, some nights almost to overflowing. God worked and quite a number got saved and added to the assemblies. I commenced there on 17th October 1948 and continued until 14th January 1949. Sometimes Irish evangelists don't take 'times or seasons' into account. While sometimes I have agreed to fixed dates and periods, I believe it's wiser to leave it so that if God is working we are free to continue.

The assembly in Ballymena, then meeting in Wellington Street Gospel Hall, asked my father and me for gospel meetings. Though my father had been preaching for many years it was his first gospel meetings in Ballymena. I was very nervous about it. I had heard so much about the large meeting and able men in it. When I arrived and saw the large hall filled, and particularly the grey-headed, dark suited elders sitting at the front, if anything, my nervousness increased.

My father said to me, "These Ballymena folk are very keen on punctuality. What would you think if we preached night about?" ie "You give out the hymns, pray and make the announcements and I'll preach. The next night we will reverse the order." This we did and in a few nights all settled to it.

In the first week two professed to be saved. Mr A Buick, one of the grey-headed elders of whom I was more or less afraid, warmly shook my hand at the door and said, "That will do." Attendances at the meetings were very good, God was pleased to bless and a number professed salvation. The meetings continued for several weeks in the gospel, and my father stayed an extra week for ministry.

A brother from Bloomfield assembly in Belfast had asked me for a Lord's day and suggested I have a ministry meeting as well as the gospel. In my simplicity I never thought anything more than just one day. The Lord's day was the first Lord's day of January 1949. I enjoyed the meetings and the day with the saints, but at the close of the gospel meeting I was asked to wait as the overseers wanted to speak to me. The correspondent speaking for his brethren said, "We would like you to come for special gospel meetings." Perhaps I shouldn't have, but I couldn't resist it! I said, "Was I here today for a trial sermon?" They simply smiled and said, "We would like you to come." I told them I had promised Ballymena, but could come after that. So it was arranged. I commenced there in mid March and was there until mid May. It was my first series in Belfast, and as usual, folks wondered about the new young preacher and came to hear. I was living in Londonderry at that time and arrangements were made for me to stay with one of the overseers, who treated me with much care and kindness. Bloomfield had then a group of spiritual, strong overseers. At that time the assembly had quite an influence on the local area and it was comparatively easy to get the neighbours in. Right from the start God moved and on the first Tuesday night a woman got saved, and on the Thursday a man got saved. This was the beginning of a nice work of grace. While dealing with Bloomfield, let me mention that these meetings were in the old hall which was getting too small, so a new hall was erected, a large comfortable building. The assembly invited me for the opening meetings on a Lord's day, ministry in the afternoon and gospel at night. God set the seal of His approval on the work. In the afternoon a man got restored and at night another got saved. Looking back over the years, we feel sad that the city assemblies, once so strong and fruitful, are finding it so uphill and difficult. One wonders why. Urban decay and population shift may account for some of it, possibly not it all. The assembly at Creeduff, Co Tyrone, was anxious that my father and I should try some gospel meetings in the area. We spent the whole summer there, six weeks in the gospel hall and six weeks in the tent at Castlegore two or three miles away, near to Castlederg town. We found little interest with the local people. I often think of a local farmer, well on in life, who standing at the door of a large hayshed said to me with tears, "When I was young Mr H Creighton and Mr Thompson Bell had meetings here and I was concerned and should have been saved, but I wasn't. God knows I'd give the farm today if I could get salvation." Though we talked with him and prayed with and for him we didn't hear of his getting to know the Saviour. God only knows where he is.

Another of the Belfast assemblies, Ballyhackamore, asked father and me for gospel meetings. He was no stranger to them. In days of problems, he with others was able to help them. The assembly was large and strong in many ways, having recovered from teaching from other areas which had greatly upset them. We were a few nights into the meetings when my father suffered another heart attack and was unable to preach. I continued the meetings, and while there was not much in the way of conversions, a number who earlier were saved got stirred up and were baptised and added to the company. I was privileged to be back in Ballyhackamore in 1966 when God worked and several professed salvation. A couple of brethren came to see me on the last night of the first series in Ballyhackamore and asked me if I would go to Rosslea in Co Fermanagh. One said, "It would do you good to get out of the city and into the country." He didn't explain why. Rosslea is situated on a finger of land, well-nigh surrounded by the Irish Republic. It was in those days a good area for smuggling! Rationing was still known in Ulster, and across the border food stuffs etc were fairly plentiful and so were visitors! A brother from the Clones assembly had a business and it was generally known that he had never smuggled a sixpence worth of anything. One of his sons had worked hard and built up a very successful grocery store and petrol station. This man, like his father, was a Christian gentleman and highly respected in the village and in the assembly. He was murdered during the troubles 1970-95. No-one was brought to justice for his killing. He was shot as he stood behind the counter in the store. When I had the meetings I was staying with the local RUC sergeant in charge of the police station. He and his good wife showed me every kindness. There were two young constables, just a few months saved, who helped me in visitations. They were well known in the district and the marked change in their lives since conversion spoke to many and gave some an interest in the gospel. One of the two constables has for several years been engaged in full-time gospel work, as has the sergeant with whom I stayed.

We had encouraging numbers of local people nightly, but we finished without hearing of anyone getting saved. Years later, a fellow evangelist, labouring in a nearby district was told by an elderly man he contacted while visiting around that he was saved at those meetings. We do well to keep in mind "the harvest is the end of the age" (Matthew 13:39) — not the end of the meetings. Then we will see the full results of our work for God.

Mr W P McVey who was preparing to go to Malaya had some meetings in the village of Sandhead, near Stranraer, and had promised to be one of the speakers at the Stranraer conference on New Year's day in 1950. As he was going abroad soon after that date, and wanted to spend this holiday season with his parents, he asked me if I would take his place and stay for a few meetings. Having promised to commence elsewhere I had only ten nights free. He said, "They will be satisfied with that." I went and at the conference spoke on "some of the tears of the Bible." One or two of the more mischievous members called me the 'weeping prophet'.

I'm very glad I stayed the ten nights. The meetings were in an old terrace house, more or less converted into a hall! In those nights God saved three who have continued steadfastly. One has been the correspondent for the small assembly for years.

I returned home to fulfil the promise I had made, but it was so different, the interest, the atmosphere etc. I really wished I had continued in Wigtownshire. I trust we learn by our mistakes. In later years I was again in that place and God gave blessing. Reference will be made to this later.

About that time I seemed to be getting invitations to other places rather than Northern Ireland. When I went preaching in 1946 I never thought of anything but staying in local areas. But now, looking back, I am glad I moved out a little. I believe it was an education to me and I trust a blessing to others. One of the old veteran preachers, Mr John Moneypenny, said to me, "I'm glad I didn't spend all my time in Ireland, don't you do it either."

A couple I knew from boyhood days had gone to live in

Kempston, Bedfordshire. The husband had taken an interest in
the assembly and was a real help. On behalf of the assembly he
asked me for gospel meetings and I felt I should go. Kempston is
near to 'John Bunyan' country, but though it is the people live in
darkness. I asked a lady one day if she would come to the gospel
meeting. She asked, "What is a gospel meeting?" I commenced
there in early 1950. The meetings continued for six weeks with
nice interest and numbers, and God was pleased to work and
reward the saints for their exercise and labour. A lady was
coming each night, and as I spoke I thought she didn't look
happy. Preachers don't have their eyes closed on the platform!
When I enquired from the saints about her, they knew her, but
had no knowledge of how she was spiritually. I thought, "When
I get a suitable opportunity I will ask her." Having a key of the
hall, and being in early, I was sitting reading the Bible when the
door opened and in she came. I welcomed her and said we were
glad to see her coming each night. "Yes," she said, "I am glad to
come." Sometimes it would hardly be wise to ask people if they
enjoyed your meetings, but I thought "I'll try." I said, "Do you
enjoy the meetings?" She looked at me and paused for a
moment, then said, "I do and I don't." I thought, "You have
opened the door, and I will go in." I asked Mrs Proctor, "Are you
a saved woman?" I think I will never forget her look and answer.
"Young man, I am in my eightieth year, and until I attended
these meetings, I thought I was on my way to Heaven, but all I
had was the good life I tried to lead. Now I have found out that I
am a lost sinner and need to be saved, and would like to be." With
that, someone came in. I slipped her a copy of the booklet, *Safety,
Certainty and Enjoyment*. As I did, she said, "Would you come down
in the morning, and if you come down at 11.00 am, the house
will be free." Next morning at 11.00 am, I pressed the bell and as
soon as she answered the door her face was shining, and a
change was visible. I said, "How are you this morning?" She
replied, "Fine! I got saved at 3 o'clock this morning. Come in and
I'll tell you. Last night when I came home from the meeting, I
took no supper and I couldn't sleep, my burden of sin was so
great. I tossed from side to side until 3.00 am when the hymn
sung so often in the meeting came to mind:

I do believe I will believe
That Jesus died for me;
That on the cross He shed His blood
From sin to set me free.

Just there I saw that Jesus had died for me and all I had to do was to turn and put my trust in Him".

About six months later, I was back for a week of ministry meetings, and the dear old lady had aged quite a bit in appearance. On the last night, making her way down the aisle with the aid of her walking stick, she firmly grasped my hand and said, "I will likely never see you again in this world, but I'll see you in Heaven, for I'm saved."

As I think of these dark and needy places I wonder why young men with gift and ability don't try to reach out to the many 'who sit in darkness'. "Can we to men benighted the lamp of life deny?"

For many years Enniskillen assembly was small and struggling, but of late years, God has blessed and they now have a good and active company. Mr S Lewis lived in Ballinamallard and was greatly interested in the Enniskillen assembly. It was in large measure as a result of his labours and that of his brother-in-law Mr D Craig, that the assembly was formed. He asked me if I would consider trying some tent meetings. I said, "I would if you will help me." We secured a piece of ground right in the centre of the town, which had been bought by some local christian businessmen with a view to commencing what has proved to be a very successful cattle mart. Our tent was in one corner, while cattle sales were going on from day to day. An auctioneer who was a believer was busy one day as we passed by, and for a minute or two we listened to him. He was having problems getting the offers he desired. Noticing us on the edge of the crowds, he called out, "Would you two preaching men buy a wee blue cow?" At least it was cheap advertising! We didn't get large meetings, but we did see some blessing in salvation, some who ever since have been interested and useful in the assembly.

One night when I was preaching I noticed a lady at the back of the tent. Her hands were moving quickly, at first I wondered if she was knitting! But no she was sitting beside a young man who was deaf and dumb, and with sign language she was giving him the message. On making enquiries, we found he was working on a temporary basis in the town. The lady was also working in the area. She was a believer from an assembly in Belfast, and she, with ourselves, had the joy of knowing that the young man had got saved.

My father was a frequent visitor to Newry, and when we were children, we were happy for him to be there! The Hagan family were in the confectionery business and each Friday night they sent boxes of sweets. Father, over the years, had seen a good deal of blessing there, and again God moved and several professed salvation when he and I were there in 1950.

A few miles south of Stranraer, there was a small assembly at Drummore. They showed interest while I was in Sandhead, and asked for some meetings in their village. I was happy to go and glad I did. While we heard of no professions, we had very good attendance and interest. All kinds of people came, farmers, business people, church elders, etc. God gave help to preach, and I would feel satisfied that something was accomplished. We will know later. That was in 1950. On returning in 1954 we found the interest was much less, and since then, the assembly has ceased to exist and the hall was sold.

A farming family, then active in Londonderry assembly, had a Sunday school in their drawing room, and it was suggested we should try a few gospel meetings. Mr B Reilly, who was saved at the tent in the Waterside, helped me and we had most encouraging meetings. The testimony of the family impressed the neighbours, and they attended well. Several were saved. It seems a pity the old-fashioned house meeting has almost ceased.

Some of the Fermanagh saints were interested in meetings in Lisbellaw and Enniskillen. I tried both places, but met with little success. Still having the district where we had the house meetings in mind I asked Mr McEwen to join me in tent meetings. We had six happy weeks there and good attendance of local people, as well as support from Donemana and Londonderry assemblies. God gave us to see souls saved and His people cheered.

Several miles from Londonderry, near Claudy, was the Straidarren assembly, formed through the labours of Mr James

Clark and Mr W McCracken. In it were a number of farmers, men whose testimony in the area was sterling, but they had moved away from the principles taught by the evangelists who saw them saved. There was a brother who was not happy about the way they were acting and from time to time would ask me to preach on the Lord's day. Being young and not too sure what to do I consulted with Mr J Stewart (evangelist). He said, "Go, and if you can drive a peg in on the right side, do it." I must say they were very nice to me, and kind. I have a Strong's Concordance with a nice inscription they gave me when I got married. Now I was preaching full time and they asked me for special meetings, so, feeling I might have better control in the tent, I suggested I would take the tent to the area. The meetings were very well attended, believers from Limavady and Donemanagh came and put their best into the effort. God worked and a nice number got saved. As the meetings were about to finish the brethren asked me if I would assist them in getting speakers for the Lord's day meetings. It was arranged we would all meet and discuss matters. They had been given to invite men, no doubt good men, but not in assembly fellowship. I was not happy about that and said if they ceased that, I would help. They all agreed to do this, and to confine themselves to brethren in assembly fellowship. I went at once to see Mr S Ussher in Garvagh. He knew of the brethren in small local business affairs, and as well, he had experiences of the same kind of assembly problems, maybe more pronounced in Killykergan, than they were in Straid. Mr Stewart, Mr McCracken and Mr McKelvey went and helped them, and ever since they have continued in scriptural ways. Knowing this, Mr Ussher said he would gladly try to be of help in Straidarren.

He was a help there and with others was able to encourage the assembly in the ways of God. It is well "to be watchful and strengthen the things that remain". It would be so easy to turn away and leave them to drift farther. Some could be helped, others we fear do not want help. The first time my father was at Killykergan, he was then just a young preacher and possibly a little rash. It was Mr J Stewart, evangelist, who took him to the conference. On the way Mr Stewart said to him, "If a woman gets up to speak here today, you keep quiet." Apparently a sister was in the habit of speaking, but wise men like Mr Stewart, Mr

McCracken and Mr McKelvey were the three involved in trying to help at that time. They did not try to cut the place off, rather they rallied around and tried to teach and help, which they were able to do. There is a difference between those who need help and will accept it, and others who will not be helped. I had all the foregoing details from my father and Mr McKelvey.

In August 1994 the assembly at Straidarren, Co Londonderry arranged a special tea meeting to mark the 100th birthday of Mrs Norris, their oldest member. They invited a number of folks and family friends from around as well as members of assemblies in the area. Because of my long-standing association with Mrs Norris I was asked to give some help along with preaching brethren. It was a very happy time and the hall was packed. Mrs Norris was presented with texts from her own assembly and the Limavady assembly gave her a Bible. Just as the meeting was about to commence an elderly gentleman came in and sat beside Mrs Norris on the front seat. She had no idea who he was. He said to her, "Are you the last of the Riley family?" "No," she said, "I have a brother Charlie in Canada who writes to me." Looking into her face he said, "I am Charlie." It was a touching scene. She had not seen him for many years and the family brought him over for the meeting. He is associated with an assembly in the Toronto area.

In the autumn of 1951 I joined Mr McEwen in Taunton, Somerset, for gospel meetings. The assembly was large and active with an exercise about the gospel. It is sad to see so many assemblies appearing to lose the zeal for the gospel, it changes many things. We had large meetings with some fruit in conversions. While in that Somerset area I had a gospel series in West Monkton, where again God graciously blessed His Word.

In that winter I had meetings in Tully, Co Antrim. Mr T McKillen, a native of that part, while in Ballymena in business had a deep concern for his old neighbours and friends, and arranged meetings in the hall there. I have had two series there and have seen some blessing. The hall has been well maintained, and a good Sunday school and monthly gospel meeting are carried on. Though Mr McKillen has gone home, his son Matthew and others carry on for God. After Tully I returned to Straidarren for ministry meetings, some who got saved at the tent were received into fellowship and it is a joy from time to time to see them happy amongst the believers.

The assembly in Newcastle, Co Down, invited Mr McEwen and myself for a gospel effort in 1952. When I told my father we were going, he said, "A short time will do you there," for it had the reputation of being a difficult area. Mr McEwen was greatly interested in the area as during World War I, he being a conscientious objector, was sent to work on Mr S Wright's farm at Ballywillwill and had often visited Newcastle and sought in song and preaching to make the gospel known. There was then no assembly in the town.

It was evident from the commencement of the meetings that there was an interest, and God worked and a nice number got saved. After that series the assembly asked if we would accept responsibility for the summer season open air meetings. This we gladly did and for twelve summers in succession we were there. We were able to use the local cinema for a late gospel meeting on Sunday evenings. The interest and blessing were most encouraging. Christians from areas around came in and helped us. We had three open air meetings each day; 4.00 pm; 7.00 pm and 10.00 pm, during which hundreds heard the gospel and we rejoiced to hear of people getting to know the Saviour.

On the outskirts of Belfast, some assembly christians from Donegal Road, Ebenezer and Matchett Street assemblies, carried on a Sunday School and gospel outreach in a wooden hall. I was there in the spring of 1952 helped by Mr R Neill who for many years has served the Lord in Africa. The teachers got the scholars and some parents to attend and there was some fruit in conversions.

In the summer of that year Mr F Bingham and I had a tent in Limavady. Our brother Fred was a devoted servant and it was a joy to labour with him and stay together in a believer's home. God honoured His Word and a few professed faith in Christ. Later that summer Mr McEwen and I went over to work in the Ayrshire tent. An evangelist from Scotland had had a few meetings in the tent erected in Mauchline and some thought we should carry on just there. After a short time we felt there was little interest in that village, but from a village a short distance away people were coming, and we felt that the tent should go there. So we made a quick move and commenced meetings in

Auchinleck. So rapid was the move that when a couple of car loads came a distance and the tent or the preachers were not to be found, some wondered about a 'partial rapture!'

The interest was good in Auchinleck and from the first night the tent was filled. I think I will never forget how heartily the believers sang the hymns, some of which I had never heard, such as 'O listen to our wondrous Story'. Many heard the gospel and some professed conversion.

At the end of that summer season, in 1952, I went to Glasgow to have gospel meetings in association with the assembly then meeting in Plantation Street, between Govan and the city centre (now meeting in Harley Street, Ibrox). In some respects in those days it was a kind of Irishman's retreat. Several of the responsible brethren and others were Irish. I enjoyed the warm hearty fellowship of the christians and it was not too difficult to get local folk in. The meetings lasted for five weeks and God saved some who were added to the assembly. When the assembly erected a fine new hall in January 1971 I was asked for another spell of gospel meetings which lasted almost eight weeks. The local interest was beyond what any of us expected and God blessed the exercise of His people and quite a number professed salvation. The annual conference meetings of the assembly at New Year were seasons to be remembered. It was a joy to be there quite often and share with ministering brethren from many parts of the UK.

In 1952 I was invited to Cardiff and Swansea for gospel meetings. Adamsdown in Cardiff was a fairly long established assembly where God had worked a good deal in earlier days, but I could see no sign of interest and I didn't hear of any blessing. God knows.

In the assembly a Fforestfach, Swansea, I had a happy time during my two or three special efforts there. Mr W Trew, who lived in Cardiff and Mr Walter Norris worked consistently in the Welsh Valleys with their tent, when I told him I was going to Fforestfach said "it was the best meeting in South Wales". Quite a number of the members were Welsh speakers. The good brother with whom I stayed told me it was Welsh they spoke in the garden of Eden. My response was, "No wonder they were put out!" The hymn book they used was in English on one side of the page and on the other side Welsh. Often they would sing a verse or two in English and then break off into Welsh, when they sang as if inspired. God blessed the visit and saved souls. I was blessed and refreshed amongst the saints.

Coming back to God's own country! (N Ireland), I had meetings in Albertbridge Road assembly in Belfast. Mr Hill (a retired sea captain) accompanied me almost daily in visitation and helped me to get people interested to come in to hear the gospel. The whole assembly rallied around the meetings. One young woman seems to stand out as I recall those days. She later became the wife of Mr J Walmsley and served the Lord with him in South America. Almost every night she had a seatful of people with her, a missionary in a true sense before she went abroad. Five or six we know of got saved.

In January 1953 I was in Annalong on the County Down coast. We had a fair bit of contact with the believers there while in the open air work in Newcastle. The brethren were excellent singers and we were always glad of their help. When Mr McEwen saw them coming, he would say, "We'll sing the prodigal today". He enjoyed the part singing of "God is calling

Bridgeport Cemetery Connecticut U.S.A.

the prodigal". The Annalong meetings were nicely attended, but with only one man getting saved. When I was in Annalong the Princess Victoria foundered in a violent storm. For days the whole coastline was alerted as they searched for bodies. A leader in the Stranraer assembly that I knew well was last seen on the deck on his knees just before she sank. Two nights earlier I had crossed on that ship, and a rough night it was, but nothing like the night she went down. One of Northern Ireland's members of the House of Commons was lost just within sight of his home on the coast. I sometimes use that in the gospel to point out that people could be near to salvation and yet be lost.

Ballymena is one of the places I have visited most in gospel meetings. One day in Belfast I met a lady I knew well who originally came from Ballymena. She asked me where I was going for meetings. I said "Ballymena." "My!" she said, "Can they get no-one else?"

My second visit was in 1953 when I was accompanied by Mr McEwen. There was a good measure of exercise and interest with the members of the assembly. Each morning at 10.30 am the businessmen and others came together to pray and it was nice to see them all kneeling together and united in the gospel. Many were in the same lines of business and while the ads in the local paper would have given the impression that they were keen competitors, their hearts were one in the things of God. God graciously gave help and blessing in a number getting saved.

One dear brother whose son was almost twenty, and declared he would soon be finished with gospel meetings, had prayed in the prayer meeting and told the Lord he was disappointed that his son was not saved. Said he, "He has heard as much gospel as would sink a ship and still no word of his salvation." That very night going out of the meeting, the young man told Mr McEwen he had got saved as the meeting went on. He and a number of others continue happily in the assembly taking part and sharing in responsibility.

The small assembly in Glassford, Lanarkshire, was anxious for some gospel meetings. I tried to fulfil their desire and help them, but the only results that were evident from the meetings were four backsliders being restored.

In June 1953 I pitched the tent at Broomhedge. I have always enjoyed working with the tent. We have found that people come more easily to tent meetings than to meetings in the gospel hall, and this was true at Broomhedge where God came in grace and blessed His Word in salvation. Later that summer Mr McEwen and I had the tent at Crossgar, but found little to encourage.

While in Kempston, Bedfordshire, in 1950 I met some from the assembly at Corby, Northamptonshire, who later wrote asking for two weeks of gospel meetings. An Irish brother in the area said, "Two weeks only? You will be asking the preacher to stay longer than that". "No," they said. "That will be long enough," but it turned out the Irishman's way. I have had three efforts in the gospel there with "signs following the preaching of the word". Corby was a new town, and the assembly was made up mostly of believers from Scotland, who had sought employment in the steel works, so from a small village it had grown rapidly to a large town.

Towards the close of 1953 my father and I had meetings in a store belonging to a Mr T Lowe, a cousin of my father. We had very good numbers and while we saw no one saved, some who got saved later spoke of being awakened at that time. In between gospel efforts I have sought to have a few ministry meetings in places where earlier God's hand had been at work. These short efforts took me to Broomhedge, Sandhead and Drummore (Wigtownshire) and Ballynahinch.

In the beginning of the following year Mr McEwen and I were at Sidcup, Kent, where the assembly meeting in Birket Hall was large and had some good spiritual leaders. The meetings were well attended and six we knew of professed salvation. One lady who was attending our meetings and was concerned, went one night to a large effort being conducted in central London and got saved. Strange, the next night a lady who had been attending in London, and was troubled, came to our meeting and got saved. I am told the assembly in Sidcup no longer exists. Problems of various kinds came in and the saints scattered.

In May of 1954 Mr Reg Jordan and I started meetings in a tent in Annbank, Ayrshire. After the opening conference, a nice brother from an assembly some miles away approached me and said, "I lead a male voice choir and we could come and help you here." I said, "That would be good, come as often as you can and join in the singing of the congregation, we will be glad to see

you." I don't know that I saw him during all the weeks of the
meetings! We had a real stirring time, good attendances,
excellent singing and help to preach. God moved, and quite a
number got saved, among them a young woman who later went
to Ethiopia as a missionary's wife. A woman who was a member
of the assembly, and took a real interest in the village folk, was
travelling in a bus from Annbank to Mossblown with Mr Jordan
and me when a drunk man got on, and looking at Mary said,
"Mary, you don't need this stuff to make you happy".

While in Corby I heard of there being no assembly gospel
work in the County of Huntingdon. When I mentioned this to
Mr McEwen, he said, "Could we try some?" We were able to get
the loan of a tent from a brother in Bedfordshire, and getting a
suitable site, we pitched it and commenced our meetings in
1954. Some believers from the Cambridge assembly (Panton
Hall) and some from Corby came and showed real interest and
fellowship in the work. The man in charge of the local library
came nightly and got to see his need. After the meeting one
night he said to us, "I have got saved. I have discovered that
what I need is in the Person of the Lord Jesus, and last night in
my room I trusted him". During our time there we were able to
get lodgings in St Ives with a couple not in assembly fellowship
who showed us "no little kindness".

The brethren in Glenburn, Belfast, had erected a hall and in
fellowship with surrounding assemblies had commenced to
break bread. They invited Mr McEwen and me for the first
effort in their hall. Mr McEwen used to say to me, "It's a kind of
shuttle service. I come over to Ireland, you come over to
England". In Glenburn we saw a little fruit that still remains.

In January 1955 Fortwilliam assembly in Belfast asked me
about a visit to their hall, and I felt I should go. It was one of the
seasons I will long remember, thirteen weeks in all. Each Friday
we had an all night prayer meeting, nights of laying hold on
God. Dear men and women who with tears and fervency waited
in God's presence. Was it any wonder that well over twenty got
saved and many of the believers spoke of God helping and
blessing them?

For many years the Largs Bible readings, held the first week in
May, proved to be of real blessing to many of us. Since being in
the Lanarkshire tent work in 1948 I was invited as a guest to

Largs Bible Readings: Mr A Borland, Mr E W Rogers.

Netherhall, where the readings were held. It was an experience and a joy to company with mature believers and Scottish, English, and Welsh evangelists, and to have seasons of prayer and to have the Scriptues opened to us by brethren H St John, E W Rodgers, A Borland, J Allen and A Leckie with several other Bible teachers taking part.

After the readings in 1955 Mr McEwen and I went down to Cornwall for tract distribution and open-air meetings. No one invited us, we were entirly on our own. It was a joy day by day to go from door to door, speak to the people and when suitable to have an open-air meeting. Assembly work in Cornwall has been very small and weak, while in the adjoining county of Devon, there were many meetings and a good measure of prosperity in the gospel.

In the autumn of that year I was again in South Wales, first of all in Carmarthen where the assembly there has grown somewhat in more recent times. In those days it was struggling, however, we were cheered with some interest and blessing. After Carmarthen I was at Llannelli, where at that time there were two halls. I was then in the smaller hall, later I was in the larger hall where there was a strong assembly work. Leaving Llanelli I moved a few miles to another assembly, at Loughor where some professed salvation. Then on to Fforestfach, where earlier I had seen God work. Again, a little blessing in salvation was seen. Looking back on it, I feel that my dear wife was very patient and courageous caring for the home and family in my long journeys away from home. This visit to South Wales lasted two months.

On coming home I had a Lord's Day in Larne, in the old hall in Pound Street. The feeling in the meeting that day caused the brethren to ask if I would consider some special gospel meetings. I felt as they did, and in two weeks the meetings commenced there. God in Grace gave us to see a real interest and quite a number professed salvation.

Early in 1956 I was in Ballynahinch. The assembly there at that time seemed to be experiencing a time of refreshing and was showing an active interest in reaching out to the town and district with the gospel. Our meetings were well attended and God was working. An aunt of my father's who in early life had left home and married a Roman Catholic, and had lived for many years in Eire, towards the close of a long life came back to County Down. A relation who influenced her to attend the meetings and brought her nightly in his car had, with us, the joy of seeing her saved. Some who were deeply troubled got saved at later meetings we had.

The assembly in Dundonald, of which I am a member, invited Mr McKelvey and me for meetings. It was my first time to be associated with that dear man of God and on this occasion God gave us to see some blessing in salvation.

Mr McEwen and I had another spell, this time in Tavistock, Devon. In earlier life he had been in business there and was appointed a trustee of the hall. All the other trustees had passed away by the time we were there. Jokingly, he used to say to me, "This is my church". The meetings were small and didn't last too long.

USA & Canada

In the early part of 1956 I was invited to visit USA and Canada. From my earliest days my father often spoke of going there as he had relations and friends who wrote to him, but somehow his visit never materialised. When I was invited and my fare paid I made up my mind to go. I sailed from Cobh, in Cork, in mid August on board a Holland American ship, the 'SS Massdam'. We had a very pleasant voyage until a day or so from New York. I was returning to my cabin in the afternoon when I met one of the stewards coming out of my room and I enquired of him what he was doing. He was a European who spoke little English. "Closing port holes," he said. I asked, "Why"? The sea was calm and there was delightful sunshine. Shrugging his shoulders he said, "Hurricane perhaps". And he was right. We had a rough night, but being a good sailor, I was not sick although many were. In the morning it was all over, and we moved calmly into New York. An American, quite excited at seeing the great skyline, said to me, "Did you ever see anything like that before? I never did". My reply to him was, "If you had never seen Ireland, you would think it was great". He appreciated the humour, and we talked until the ship tied up. I couldn't find one believer in all the hundreds aboard. Mr G.N. Reager, a well known evangelist, with his wife met me and took me to their home in Philadelphia. I had my first ministry meeting in Olney. Quite a number of 'old country folk' were present and we talked much after the meeting. The next night I was in Bryn Mawr where again many Irish folk attended. A brother praying before the ministry said to the Lord, "Thanks for giving the preacher journeying mercies and bringing him into our midst. You know, Lord, some Irishmen have come and been a great blessing to us, but you know Lord it would have been better if some had stayed at home". I looked up and wondered. I learned after the meeting that he was Mr Roger Greer, a brother who as a boy was saved when Mr Robert Love was preaching in Newtownhamilton, Co Armagh. Roger became a good and kind friend to me. On the last Lord's day I was there, Mr Greer praying at the close of the remembrance meeting thanked God for the gospel meetings and then commended me to God. He said, "You know Lord, every time we think of him we will remember the text, 'whose son the stripling is' " (1 Samuel 17:56).

Mr Reager and I set off the next day to go to Sault Ste Marie, Ontario, for gospel meetings, the journey being about 1000 miles. This was not much to folk there, but coming from Ireland, to me it was big! We called in at Midland and Owensound with a ministry meeting in both. At Owensound we were joined by Mr Ernest Sprunt, a Canadian evangelist. The journey was pleasant and interesting and we soon arrived in 'the Soo' (that's what they call the Sault Marie). We were made very welcome in the home of Dr Sam West where we stayed for the duration of the meetings. The conference at the first weekend was large and profitable. Most of the speakers I had never met or heard before, save one, Mr John Norris who had just arrived in Canada. We saw several profess salvation at the meetings and I left happy having made friends of several. My wife had a brother living in Port Arthur (now Thunderbay). I wanted to see the family so it was arranged that I should have a week of ministry there. On the plane there I felt the meetings should be gospel. As I was greeted at the airport, a brother said, "We wonder should the meetings be gospel". Telling him of my thought, we decided to preach the gospel and it was well we did. There was blessing in salvation. It was nice to notice the assemblies are not booked up so hard and fast as elsewhere and they can easily fit in meetings.

I had a brother 13 months younger than I who met his death while on training exercises with the RAF at North Battleford, Sask. I was desirous to visit his grave and if possible meet some who knew him. After I left Port Arthur I had a few nights in Winnipeg, taking in their Fall conference. After that I had a short visit to Portage La Prairie and Taylorside. From Taylorside a brother flew me into North Battleford in the private plane he used for his business. Not being accustomed to these small planes I wasn't too sure. As we retired at night the brother said to me, "If it's a nice clear morning we'll go just after breakfast". I went to bed hoping the morning would not be suitable, but when I awoke the sun was shining and the morning good. After breakfast, my friend said, "Bring your case over to that field, and I'll get you there". So off we went. I enquired of him, "how safe the small plane was with only one engine...If it fails, what happens?" "Wait," said he, "and I'll show you." Switching the engine off, we glided down to a large prairie section (620 acres). As soon as we landed a farmer came rushing out on his tractor enquiring, "What is wrong?" "Nothing," said my pilot, "I'm just bringing an Irishman down to see how we can glide to safety in case of engine failure." I gave the farmer some tracts and we were soon airborne.

After seeing the grave, but with no success re friends of my brother, I had a couple of nights in Calgary and then Vancouver where I stayed with Mr and Mrs George Campbell, who made my arrangements in that part. I had meetings in Cedar Cottage, South Maine, Woodland, Fairview and North Vancouver. Then I moved on to Arlington and Seattle from where I went by train to Chicago. Then on to Detroit for the conference and a few nights where I was lovingly cared for by Mr and Mrs Barr. Mrs Barr had been a good friend to my mother and was kind to our family when we were quite young. Mr Frank Knox was at Detroit conference and in good form. Speaking one day he made reference to 'Big Jim', a leader amongst other christians. Some thought at first it was me! But he soon fixed that up.

The Bryn Mawr conference was the next weekend, and it was an enjoyable season. Another Irish preacher joined me there, Mr H Paisley. He and I shared the conference gospel meeting at which two professed conversion. After the conference I was in Toronto for two weeks, then to Boston for further nights of ministry. Whilst I was there I stayed with my uncle and aunt who were in an assembly in the city. I was glad to get back to Bryn Mawr and Mr Reager's home as I was tired travelling and from nightly meetings. After a few quiet days at Christmas 1956 I was on the move again, up to Montreal for their conference at New Year. There it was bitterly cold and with quite a snowfall. The conference was good and profitable. Still another Irish preacher joined us, Mr Charles Fleming whom I had known since early boyhood, and who had often preached with my father. Some years later I visited him in hospital in Toronto and was saddened to see him lying in bed helpless. Soon after that God called him home. One afternoon God gave help in

preaching from Isaiah 40 on 'the greatness of God'. Mr D
Leathem gave out the hymn 'How great Thou art'. I can still see
beloved brother Mr Tom Wilkie sing with tears coursing down
his checks.

Getting back from Montreal we had meetings in Longport,
Patterson, Kearney, New York, and a brief visit to Richmond,
Matoaca and Petersburg, in Virginia. At the Bryn Mawr
conference two sisters said to me, "Why not have some gospel
meetings?" Following prayer it was arranged to commence in
mid January 1957.

Mr Reager, who had been unwell and not able for meetings,
came each night and opened the meetings. God gave quite a
good interest, good numbers attended and souls were saved,
some of whom had been long prayed for. Going out one night a
young lady spoke to me and at once I detected an Irish accent.
Chatting to her I found she came from County Fermanagh and
lived not far from the gospel hall in Ballinamallard, but she said
she had never been in it. I enquired if she was saved and she said,
"No, but I would like to be". I encouraged her to come nightly,
which she did, and both she and her sister got saved as well as
some others. That young lady has taken a real interest in divine
matters, spending some time in Zambia, later getting married
and settling back in Ireland. We had the joy of seeing some of her
family profess salvation at recent meetings. While still in the
USA she wrote asking me if I would consider some meetings in
her home district, as she was concerned about her parents and
the large family. Later we will see about the outcome.

Back in the UK

While in Vancouver and getting near the time to return to Ireland, I was wondering just what to do in the way of meetings when I got home. A Lord's Day in July before I went to the USA in August, I had been with the assembly in Letterkenny and enjoyed the sense of God's presence in the place and was happy to see a good-sized gospel meeting. I felt a visit there might prove fruitful, so I wrote to Mr H McKinney, a christian gentleman and a beloved brother, who a few years later passed away very suddenly and was greatly missed in the assembly and district. I told him of my feelings. He wrote back and said, "As to numbers we have little to offer, but we are trying a few Sunday evening meetings in a farmhouse, if you would care to come you would be very welcome, but it would be like Philip leaving

Samaria and going to the desert!" Nevertheless I felt I should go. After six months travelling and preaching on the American continent, I was weary and thought two or three quiet weeks would be good, but it didn't turn out that way. In all, there were sixteen weeks of meetings with real interest and quite a number saved, some of whom were added to the assembly and have given real joy.

It was nice to stand at the farmhouse, which was on a hill, and see the people coming, some on foot and some on bicycles. The local brethren said that on nights we had 140 packed into the house, and possibly 100 of them not saved. The memory of it makes one wish they were young again and could see scenes like these repeated.

After the July holiday season of that year Mr McEwen and I tried some tent meetings in Strabane, where we experienced a little blessing in salvation. Apart from Ballymena, Strabane is a place I have visited in special meetings much more than others, at times seeing blessing, at others, finding it difficult.

anfairfechan.

Mr Jack Gray, who was commended by the Frances Street assembly in Netownards to the work of the Lord in Canada, was to have a gospel series in Frances Street. I was asked to join him. The first two weeks we had the hall full, then a flu epidemic hit the town and our attendances were severely affected. But still God worked and souls were saved.

Later that year I was in Shieldhill, Falkirk, and had a happy month declaring the glad tidings with signs following.

Just after that I was in Chorley in Lancs where a young Irish doctor, whose wedding service I conducted, arranged for me to have gospel meetings with the assembly. A few years prior to that the assembly was formed as the result of gospel work in which Mr Fred Whitmore took an active part. The doctor and his wife made me feel very much at home, and having a good testimony amongst his patients, he was able to get them to attend the meetings. Again, in the goodness of God, we saw souls saved and the saints encouraged.

The assembly in Omagh invited me for gospel meetings in 1958. I arranged for Mr J Gray to join me, although he was only able to stay part of the eight weeks as he was due to go back to Canada. Mr Rodgers and Mr Beattie both lived in Omagh and for many years it was a centre for gospel and ministry meetings. The smaller assemblies in the area took an interest and the believers came and brought their families and friends, and God worked in salvation. Some saved in those meetings are now prominent and active in assembly life.

After Omagh I went on alone to Cookstown, another centre of gospel work for many years. We had nice numbers and interest, some were saved — among them a young man now engaged in full time gospel work in Northern Ireland. It gives me much joy to think of several who got saved and are now in full time service in different parts of the world. Mr J.K. Duff, for many years an esteemed servant of God, said to me, "Jim, if you and I had stayed in business and made a million pounds we would have to leave it all here. Isn't it nice to think of something for God and the world to come." When Mr W Kelly was offered an important post in Dublin University and turned it down, the professor said, "If you accepted and came here, you would make a name for yourself in the world". In reply Mr Kelly said, "Sir, of which world do you speak?" The Saviour said, "Whosoever shall lose his life for my sake, and the gospel's, the same shall save it" (Mark 8:35).

After Cookstown I was again with Mr McEwen in tent meetings in Rishton, Lancashire, and in open air meetings in Newcastle, as well as some ministry meetings in Letterkenny and Londonderry. Then I sought to fulfil the wish of the young lady who was saved in Bryn Mawr, Philadelphia, and had meetings in the hall at Ballinamallard. Excellent numbers attended and quite a few professed salvation. Though I took an interest in the young lady's family, and they came, we didn't see any of them saved, although some of them got saved at later meetings in the area. In all, the meetings lasted ten weeks which brought me to the end of 1958. The local church minister was opposed to our meetings and used to stand in the school opposite and watch who came. A lady who was attending our meetings and was a saved person was concerned about her position and where she should be. I was trying to help her and eventually she was baptised and received into the assembly and was a faithful member as long as she lived. All this raised a problem for me. I had arranged to be with a certain assembly for a month's meetings. To my dismay, I saw from the local paper that they were having men preaching who were not in assembly fellowship. No doubt good men, but that was not the point. I remonstrated with the elders pointing out that I was endeavouring to get some out of the religious systems and they were linking the assembly with such systems. I felt it was not consistent for me, in one place teaching and practising separation, and in another condoning the opposite. So I asked to be freed from my promise, to which they agreed, and we parted on good terms.

The assembly in Donegall Road, Belfast, one of the older assemblies in the city, sought help in the gospel and meetings commenced early in January 1959. The first Monday night of the meetings, I had just arrived home when I had a phone call from one of the elders telling me his son got saved as the meeting progressed. He was the first of quite a number. Nightly the hall was filled as well as the Sunday afternoons, when we tried to give some help in ministry. With urban decay, and general conditions in the area, the assembly has become small, but it is still happy and active in the gospel amongst young and old.

After some ministry meetings in Larne, and a month in Burnley, Lancashire, Mr Sam Jardine and I commenced tent meetings in Londonderry, This was my first, indeed my only opportunity to labour with Mr Jardine. He had been a prominent Baptist pastor for several years, but New Testament assembly truth reached his heart, and at quite a cost, he left his many friends and until his homecall was happy in assembly fellowship. He was a christian gentleman, a keen student of the Scripture and an acceptable speaker. I enjoyed his company as we read, prayed and preached together. God gave some blessing in salvation, and some of those saved at that time are still in assembly fellowship in Londonderry, where numbers are now very small.

After another happy series on the promenade in Newcastle with Mr McEwen, I returned to Burnley, Lancs, for gospel meetings. Those who have tried gospel work in England (sad to say few from Ireland do) know how great is the indifference and darkness, and it gets greater as days go by. However, I was happy day by day to visit, give out tracts and invite people to the meetings. Some came and heard the gospel and one or two professed conversion. Mr Beattie, who was a full time worker in Northern Ireland, said to me as we had meetings together, "Jim, we were not sent to save the people, we were sent to preach the gospel to them". I often ponder these words. Back in Ireland again I had a nice happy spell in Holywood where again God was pleased to save.

Several times I was asked for meetings in Portadown, but never seemed to see the way clear. I had arranged to commence in Growell, Co Down, when I heard that Dromore was to have meetings. These districts are quite near to each other and I have always tried to avoid starting if there were other meetings nearby, so I asked the Growell brethren if they would wait until later. I prayed and wondered what I should do and I felt impressed to phone the Portadown folks, and the answer I got was, "We are just waiting for someone to come". I said, "I'll commence next week", to which they replied, "Give us another week", which I did. The meetings began in mid November 1959 and continued until mid January 1960. It is good to hear from them, and to see in various places, some who got saved at that time. In late January I fulfilled my promise to Growell and commenced in the gospel. Growell is a long established assembly, and when I was there some of the members were very old men who vividly remembered Mr H Ferguson, the motor magnate, whose invention of the tractor was such a boon to the farming community world-wide. In early days he had been in assembly fellowship in Growell. Calling one day to see one of these old men, I asked how he was. He said, "I am well and climbing Zion's mountain and will soon be at the top". It was a joy to be amongst these believers and God gave some fruit in the gospel that still remains.

The assembly at Sidcup, Kent, had requested a further spell in the gospel. This time I was alone, the meetings were larger than my first visit, and six we heard of professed salvation. From there I went to Barrow in Furness, but found little to encourage. Mr S Thompson, Knockbracken, and I pitched the tent at Ballystockart, a short distance from Comber, where we saw a little move in salvation. I have noticed that different kinds of blessing come from meetings! At these meetings, a brother from quite a distance met a nice local girl and later they became man and wife and God has made them a blessing.

The assembly at Canley, Coventry, desired help in the gospel and I arranged to go. There were several assemblies in that city. Canley was of more recent origin and on the outskirts of the city. There I enjoyed preaching the gospel and the believers seemed to be greatly exercised about the vast need. The neighbours attended well and there were a number of professions. I had a unique experience there. After I came home I received a letter signed by all the responsible brethren, expressing appreciation for the straightforward gospel messages. In all the many places I visited, I preached as I would have done in Ireland as I feel it would be dishonourable to change the preaching to suit the circumstances or to please the people.

After Coventry I was in Warrington, Lancs, in the Foster Street assembly, a large established assembly guided and helped by godly overseers. I found it difficult to make much progress in the gospel, but the seed was sown at the doors and from the platform.

Bandon in County Cork is one of the assemblies in the

Republic of Ireland that God has richly blessed and used in the spread of the gospel in that very needy part. There I had a short series in October/November 1960, when some got saved and still continue in assembly fellowship. The assembly asked for Bible readings on the Lord's Day afternoons so I took up such subjects as the local church, breaking of bread etc. A young woman whose father was an elder in the assembly and a good man, said to me after one of the Bible readings, "Now I know why we do as we do". This made me wonder if in many cases we fail to point out these simple New Testament matters, not condemning this and that, but being positive.

Letterkenny was again visited and meetings held in their hall, with still some further blessing in salvation.

So I commenced alone in Central Hall, Bangor, in January 1961. For some years it had been considered a difficult place, and I was hesitant at first to go, but I'm glad I went. The hall was full from the first night, there was a real exercise with the assembly members, prayer meetings were well attended and it was evident that there was a spirit of expectancy. In grace, despite all our conscious weakness, the Spirit's power was known and we had a season of visitation and blessing. Some saved at those meetings are now leaders in other assemblies.

After Bangor Mr R Beattie and I were invited to Cregagh Street, Belfast. It has been my privilege and pleasure to have shared in meetings with many of the Lord's servants, at least 24 of them. I have profited in this as I prayed with them and listened to them preach. With Mr Beattie at that time, some were saved and the assembly encouraged. Like a number of other city assemblies, the numbers have dwindled and they are now much weaker, but carry on courageously in the gospel and with their annual Christmas Day conference.

In an asembly in Derby, England, there was an Irish brother enthusiastic in the gospel, who asked me if he could get the local assemblies to unite in a gospel series, would I go to preach? The effort was arranged, but like most English series, it was short, from Sunday to the following Thursday week. On the Tuesday of the second week I had an evening meal with one of the overseers, whom I considered to be a spiritual man. After thanks was given he sighed and said, "You know brother Hutchinson, when it comes to near the end of the mission you get very tired!" I said, "Dear brother, if we had you in Ireland we would kill you".

In the early summer of 1961, Mr R Jordan and I tried tent meetings in association with the Lessans assembly where, while one or two professed, we found the going difficult.

Later that summer I had meetings in Drumaness, where for many years faithful saints carried on a very good children's work. This series of meetings was one of the most encouraging for some time. About 20 professed to be saved, which gave joy to those who for years had sown the seed.

Chorley in Lancs was tried again, but with little success. Another visit to Corby, Northants, gave much more cheer in fruit in the gospel. Strathaven in Lanarkshire I found to be uphill and with little interest.

Ormeau Road Gospel Hall, Belfast, arranged meetings and I commenced in early November 1961 and had the joy of seeing the Lord working. While I was there a man asked to speak with me. He said, "I want you to tell me if I am saved". I replied, "I wouldn't be in a position to do that, but tell me your experience". He said, "I have told the men here and they don't seem to think I'm saved." His story was, "I was out of work and unwell and feeling very depressed and lonely. When near to Christmas I put on the TV to watch a nativity play, then going to bed I had a dream, and in that dream I saw a face and the person said, 'I died for thee'. Getting up in the morning all I could think of was 'I died for thee'. The more I thought about it, the more I said, 'Who died for me?' During the day, I realised the Lord Jesus died for me and I trusted Him as my Saviour". What seemed to put the brethren off was the TV and the dream. Time proved the man was really saved, and until years later when he passed away, all were confident he had got divine life. "God moves in a mysterious way."

I was in Ballymena again in the beginning of 1962 and had fair meetings. I am so thankful that in all my frequent visits to that favoured town, it still seems to have some of the spirit of the 1859 revival which began quite near to them. After Ballymena I had my first visit to Skibbereen, Co Cork. The brother who arranged for my visit also arranged that I should stay in one of the local hotels, where in many ways I was comfortable and well cared for, but I missed the Christian fellowship, especially at nights after the meetings. But I was able to sit at a nice turf fire and do quite a bit of reading. There was a nice interest and I was able to visit in many of the farmhouses for miles outside the town. In those days it was a quiet town and the people easy going. I have a nice coloured slide I took while there, depicting the main street where there was a 'no waiting' sign. A man from the country came in with his donkey and cart. Tying the donkey to the 'no waiting' sign, he proceeded to do some shopping! I have been back in the assembly there on several occasions and happy to see God working and people saved. The assembly has been blessed with godly overseers, who have guided the saints and encouraged younger men as they came forward.

When I was a younger man living in Banbridge I was quite often in Dromore to share in the gospel meeting on Lord's Day evening. The assembly there was very small and struggling but over a period of years God has blessed in a real way and now the assembly is strong and there is a vibrant gospel spirit prevailing. After Skibbereen in 1962, I had seven or eight weeks of gospel meetings, with most encouraging attendance and several getting saved, fruit that still remains in the assembly.

The assembly in Victoria Hall, Blackburn, Lancs, was one of the older English assemblies where a number of really good solid men were leaders. They invited me for gospel meetings and just after Dromore I went there. It was the first of many happy visits for their conference and gospel work. I look back with thanksgiving to God working and a number being blessed for eternity.

An Irish brother living in Southall, London, was anxious for gospel meetings in the assembly there. The place has been called 'Little Calcutta' because so very many Indian people live there. I didn't find it easy to visit among them — friendly enough, but not in any way interested in the gospel. Nevertheless, we had fairly good numbers and some blessing in salvation.

In the summer of 1962, I was with the Ayrshire tent, pitched at Springside, not far from Kilmarnock. In some series a particular hymn seems to be a favourite. This time it was, "When peace like a river". I shall not soon forget those dear Scottish saints singing their parts. There was quite a sense of God's presence and one night I closed the meeting in the usual way and not one person moved to leave. Mr McEwen and Mr Jack Hunter were visiting the tent that night and when the people still sat on, I called on these good men to come up and tell us how they were saved. Even then folk were loath to leave. God's presence was very real. Some professed conversion and were added to assemblies in the area as there was no assembly at Springside. I had lodgings there with an elderly widow and would not know how she was spiritually, but she was very kind to me.

Two assemblies in Canada invited me for meetings, Bracondale in Toronto and South Main in Vancouver. In Bracondale I was joined by Mr G Reager where we had a reasonably good effort with some professing salvation. In South Main I was joined by Mr S Maxwell, and had a very fruitful time. I enjoyed the company and fellowship of these dear servants of the Lord. They were different in many ways, but both were very good to the visiting Irish preacher. I was privileged to visit other areas for some nights of ministry; Boston, Lynden (Washington), Bryn Mawr, Arlington, Forest Grove, Fort Lauderdale, Key West, Winnipeg, Miami, Sault St Marie, Bridgeport, Detroit, Abbotsford, Portage, Montreal and New York.

Open Air Meeting, Newcastle.

Some kind folk encouraged be to stay on the American continent, but while I enjoyed all my visits I was satisfied God would have me live in Ireland. Going home, I was back in Ballygigan with good numbers and several nice cases of salvation. Then another summer season in Newcastle with three open air meetings each day and a late gospel meeting in the local cinema on Sunday nights. I used to be amused at some folk who would say, "Are you enjoying your holidays?" One elderly overseer from an assembly some miles away, who perhaps was a little critical of our work there, had occasion to be in the town, and came and stood with us on very warm days. He later said to a friend, "These men are to be commended for the work they are doing".

The large assembly then meeting in Apsley Street Hall, Belfast, the first place my father ever broke bread, invited me for meetings. The company had doctors, lawyers, business folk etc, and I wondered how my plain forthright preaching would suit them. To be fair to them, some of these professional people were the best supporters we had. The attendances were good and we had very good prayer meetings, and God wrought in salvation.

While in Vancouver with Mr S Maxwell having gospel meetings, I had a letter from the Toronto assemblies asking if I would give some help in a united effort in the city in October 1963. Thirteen assemblies agreed to suspend all their gospel work for three weeks in the local halls and hire the Queen Elizabeth Theatre and try meetings. This was a big matter and gave me a good deal of prayerful thought before I consented to go. I was joined by Mr Maxwell.

There was a good deal of talk about it all. Some said, "Spending so much money?" However a veteran Canadian evangelist, Mr H Harris, told them one night in a ministry meeting..."Instead of going off to Florida, put the dollars into the gospel"...which they did. Others said, "Why have two Irishmen?" The same evangelist said, "It wouldn't matter who you would bring, even if you brought angels it wouldn't satisfy all." Then he added, "I'd rather have angels myself than Irishmen!"

Prior to the opening meeting, we two preachers were together and between praying and wondering we spent a few

Bryn Mawr Conference, 1963. Left to right: Mr McBain; Mr McCullough; Mr Hutchinson; Mr Warke; Mr Knox; Mr W Ferguson.

anxious hours. But all our fears were groundless. The interest in the prayer meetings and the attendance were excellent. One night in the first week a business man got saved, his wife was already saved. As they embraced and wept, one of the convenors said to me, as he was deeply stirred with emotion, "To see that, it is worth all the money we spent." God gave a real harvest of souls. Some today labouring in other lands were saved at that time, and many in the local assemblies continue happily. That was the first united effort, several have been held since. One night after the gospel meeting, Mr A Joyce, himself a much used evangelist, said to me, "I can't see why any should find fault with that. I wish I was preaching in it myself." His former preaching partner, Mr T Wilkie, sat and wept as he with other full-time labourers 'saw the grace of God'.

In 1946, Banbridge assembly, in which I was brought up, shared in my commendation to full time service. Several times I had thought I would like to have a gospel effort with them. The way opened up, in January 1964 meetings commenced and continued for ten weeks. The attendance was beyond my expectation, and I was so thankful to see God working in my own town. A nice number professed conversion and many of the townsfolk came in to hear the gospel. It was decided to hire the local Temperance Hall for a late Sunday night meeting. This was filled to capacity and during that meeting some got saved. I was only a local boy, and how kind God was to give His approval to the exercise.

After Banbridge I was invited to Ebenezer Hall, Belfast, which at an earlier time was one of the large and fruitful city assemblies. I enjoyed being with them and they heartily supported the meetings. We saw a few profess salvation and the saints seemed to be encouraged.

In the early summer, soon after Ebenezer, Mr R Jordan and I joined in tent meetings associated with Bloomfield assembly. We had good tent weather and the people attended well. Like Ebenezer, Bloomfield was an active, fruitful assembly, though smaller than Ebenezer. Again, in grace, God visited us and souls were saved. The months of July and August of that year were spent in open air work in Newcastle — nice to think that in all twelve summers spent there, we heard of some getting saved each year.

In 1964 the saints in Newry asked if we would try a few meetings in their hall, which we were happy to do, and after ten weeks with them, were very thankful we had gone. God was gracious to us and created interest and gave us to see not only excellent numbers, but quite a number getting saved. After eight weeks Mr McEwen had to return home and I carried on alone. I had a unique experience there. I was not clear to close the meetings, but the elders were. This was the only time in all my years of preaching that I was asked to finish. A couple were coming each night and were deeply concerned. They came from the Ballykeel and Mourne area and I was loath to leave them. Having announced the meetings would close on the Lord's Day, I rang Mr Sam Bingham to ask if he would be at the meeting on Friday night. It was his wife who answered the phone. Quickly she said, "Will he bring Jim Cousins (another older brother) with him?" At the meeting I suggested to them that I felt I should have some meetings in their hall in view of the interest of the couple. They heartily agreed and I finished in Newry on Lord's Day and commenced in Ballykeel on the Monday. Events proved that the Newry brethren were right, for God not only saved the young couple, but several others, some who have since gone on and become leaders in other assemblies. I felt I should write to the Newry oversight and assure them that they were right and I was wrong! Early in the Newry meetings, I had to miss a night as at the close of my meetings in Holborn, Bangor, the brethren asked me if they got permission to have a radio broadcast of their Sunday evening meeting, would I be responsible to speak? I said, "I would if it was a straightforward gospel meeting." I don't like frills and curtailment. In August 1964 they told me the meeting was arranged for 13th September, which was my birthday! There were some who took exception to me doing this, largely because they were ill-informed and they thought this and that was the case, where it was nothing of the sort. I had one meeting with the BBC agent, principally to test my voice with the equipment. He asked me, "Do you read your sermons or just preach them?" I said, "I just preach." "Well," said he, "that's what we want, a 'brethren' gospel meeting." No choirs, no solos. The only thing I was tied to was time. He said, "We will flash a green light for you to start, and a red one to stop." I said, "Leave out the red one, I'll stop on time", which I did. Holborn

Hall was packed and the only difference I could see from the usual Sunday meeting was a small device on the desk, and a wire leading to the BBC van parked at the side of the hall. The BBC told me I had a listening audience of two and a half million. I had letters from various parts of the UK and Irish Republic, telling of hearing the message. Several wrote to tell us of being saved.

In January of 1965 I was in Kirkintilloch in Scotland for a gospel series. While meetings were not large, there was some interest and blessing in salvation. After that I was back in Fortwilliam, Belfast. They had erected a lovely new hall as they had outgrown the old one in which God had worked on several occasions. There was a measure of interest, but not what we had seen on the previous visit, but still God blessed His Word and several professed salvation. A week after these meetings I returned to Strabane. The assembly there was a good size and they got numbers in to their gospel meetings. Now, as I write, the assembly is very small and weak, but faithful and interested in the gospel work. We saw some fruit and the saints were encouraged.

About that time I had a week of ministry meetings in Newtownards, Limavady and Sion Mills. I had an exercise about tent meetings at Killinchy, Co Down. I met Mr McKelvey at Ballymacashon conference, and in conversation he asked where I intended to labour? I told him of my thought and it was left there. Later that evening he said, "Who will join you for this effort?" I said, "I have no-one arranged." The way he asked the question and looked at me I said, "Would you like to join me?" Gently and carefully he said, "I think I would". That commenced a most happy and fruitful association which lasted for eighteen years until he was called home. In those years I learned much from his godliness and wide experience. In all the years we never had a wrong word between us and I thank God for 'every remembrance of him'. In a variety of ways Satan sought to hinder the tent meetings starting, but God overruled and we saw a harvest of souls. Many not given to attending gospel meetings as well as several of the Christians' families got saved.

Mr Gordon Reager, an evangelist from the USA, was in Ulster for a visit. He and I shared some tent meetings at Dundonald and later we were in Peterhead for a month in the

Cleveland, USA, 1977; J G Hutchinson and Mr T McKelvey

gospel, and then visited assemblies in the Moray Firth for ministry, Lossiemouth, Cullen, Sandend, Gardenstown, and Aberdeen.

We found Scotland a cold 'country'. We had severe snow and ice, but the saints were very warm-hearted and kind. As we left we heard them say "Haste ye back". I have been several times, but Mr Reager never was back.

Coming home I started in Kingsbridge assembly in Belfast. It saddens one to write of these assemblies which then were large and active, and now are small and weak. Another time in grace God helped and meetings were well attended with a nice number professing to be saved. It is good to see them still going on, although some have gone home.

For years I had corresponded with Mr S H Moore, a former colleague of my father. He encouraged me, if I could, to make a visit to South Africa for gospel meetings. He had laboured diligently there for years seeing people saved and assemblies formed. In February 1964 I left for South Africa and had the pleasure of Mr Tom Rea's company from London to Nairobi.

Arriving in Capetown I was warmly welcomed and taken to Mr
and Mrs Moore's home, where I was privileged to stay for
several weeks. I thought South Africa a delightful country and
the climate so very nice. In all, I spent five months there.

I had several weeks of gospel meetings with the Crawford
assembly. All Mr Moore would do was to join me in the
visitations and open the meetings each night with a hymn and
prayer, save one night when, a kind couple had treated me to
lobster, I was as sick as could be. I have learned that shellfish of
any kind does not suit me at all. God blessed in the gospel and
several professed salvation, mostly 'white people'. In other
places we had good numbers of coloured folk, in those days they
had much more interest than the white population. I was
enabled to have gospel meetings in Port Elizabeth, Johannesburg
and Bulawayo, in each seeing some fruit in the gospel. I was
happy to go to Worcester where Mr Fred English laboured and
saw a good solid work, the assembly in that town and also in
Robertstown being formed.

They had their annual conference and I was arranged to speak
with Mr S Slosh and Mr Moore. A truly happy day with that nice
company of coloured believers, all desiring to be helped in divine
matters. On my way home from Bulawayo I had several days in
Zambia with Mr Charlie Geddis, who was very kind and helpful.
He took me to meet several of the other assembly workers as
well as keeping me busy in meetings; mornings, afternoons and
nights! It was enlightening to see the work there in its different
aspects. Later I felt I should have stayed longer but, being five
months away, I was anxious to get home. Since Mr James
Geddis, Charlie's father, tried to encourage me to join them
there, I have often prayed for the work, and was happy to see
some of it.

Coming home I had a week of ministry meetings in Omagh
and then commenced in the gospel in Ballyhackamore assembly,
Belfast, where I was encouraged in six weeks meetings with
good attendance and a number professing conversion. It is sad
to see that the once large and active assembly there is so reduced
in numbers and strength.

In 1966 the believers in the Crosskeys assembly were able to
get the use of the Glebe Orange Hall and invited Mr McKelvey
and myself for meetings. In many ways it was an interesting

hall, if one had gone in not knowing it was a hall used by 'Orange brethren' they would have thought it was 'Christian brethren' that used it! All around the walls were lovely gospel texts. The people attended very well and God gave help and blessing. One night as we sang the closing hymn a man left his seat at the back and came to the front seat. As soon as the hymn was finished he kneeled at the seat and cried out, "Men, pray for me, I am a lost sinner." Soon God saved the dear man and his wife also professed. She worked for a lady in the district, whose husband was a man of importance in the country. When her mistress asked her to come on a Lord's Day to make jam, she said, "No, on the first day of the week, the disciples came together to break bread, and that's where I am going". "All right," said the lady of the house, "we'll make it on Monday".

A number in the area professed conversion and it was thought wise to have some ministry meetings in the nearby Ballybollan Gospel Hall. The Christians in the area responded well and it was felt that the meetings were well worthwhile.

Annbank in Ayrshire was my next effort. I had, as mentioned earlier, happy association with the Ayrshire assemblies and it was pleasant to be with them again and further see God working in the Gospel.

The Londonderry assembly had erected a nice hall and asked Mr R Beattie and me for the opening gospel meetings. Over many years he was a frequent and favourite visitor to the assembly. I had been there for 10 years in assembly fellowship, so we were no strangers. The new building seemed to attract folks and our numbers were good, with a number getting saved. It would be nice to see God visiting there again and His work revived in that large city. Recently in the Londonderry area I was told of interesting happenings in that hall. The small assembly had moved to a new hall in the Waterside. Outside the hall there is a large notice, "The Donegall and Derry Christian Fellowship". It seems that about 40 converted Catholics use the hall and are trying to carry out the teaching of the Word of God. When one asked them, "What do you practice?" they held up a Bible and said, "All we see that this book teaches". After that effort five or six weeks were spent in Enniskillen, Crosskeys, Ballykeel, Bangor, and Mitcham Junction (London). A couple living in Daventry (the lady was Irish) encouraged me to try some gospel meetings, which I did, but with no outward signs of blessing.

In the Autumn of that year, 1967, Mr McKelvey and I went to Shanaghan, a country assembly. The hall was situated on the top of a hill in that good farming district, an assembly that over the years had been blessed and had seen people saved. We were favoured with a sense of divine help, God in grace saving a nice number and encouraging the Christians.

I paid a visit to South Wales and had gospel meetings in Loughor and Cardiff. While in a number of places in the UK I didn't see much done, I am glad that I was able to go and only God knows the outcome of daily visitation, gospel tracts and preaching, as well as seeking to help the believers. In many of these places the labourers are few. I have often thought of young men in Ulster with gift and desire to preach (I hope an 'urge', not an 'itch'), if they could see the cities, towns and villages, in many cases with little if any gospel activity, and launch out. God who supports and maintains dear brethren in foreign lands, could use them and meet their every need. I doubt if some cases of departure from truth is a valid reason for not trying.

I had an invitation from Newtownbreda assembly on the outskirts of Belfast where the hall is in a growth area. Newtownbreda assembly was a hive-off from Kingsbridge and they stll work together in happy fellowship. I had almost eight weeks with them and several professed conversion, some who now, almost every Lord's Day, engage in gospel preaching.

I paid another visit to Annalong, a small village on the main coast road around the mountains of Mourne. One of the outstanding features of that assembly was their singing. One of their overseers had perhaps one of the best singing voices I have been privileged to hear. The testimony of that village was good and being saved was a reality to the villagers. Some professed at the meetings.

Mullafernaghan assembly asked Mr McKelvey and me for meetings in 1968. This has been a place of many visitations in blessing. The only time we were free to commence was early June, but the brethren said, "It's about the worst time for us for meetings". As we were not free later we said, "We'll leave it for now". Then our brethren said, "If you can't come later, come in

June". So we started. Despite harvesting and holidays the people came and God gave us a real time of blessing. As we were closing the brethren said, "We will never again say it is a bad time. If it's God's time, that is all that matters". A short time after the meetings, on one Lord's Day, fourteen were received into the assembly. To God be the glory, He giveth the increase. During the remaining weeks of the summer and early autumn some further weeks of ministry, were held in Limavady, Dundonald, Antrim, Aughavey, and Enniskillen. Feeling that I should give to God as much time as I should give to an earthly employer, I have sought to keep fully occupied, "redeeming the time".

In the early winter Mr McKelvey and I started in Ballymagarrick. The meetings began in mid-October 1968 and continued until almost the end of January the following year. I know that some say we regard neither times nor seasons, but we believe if God is working, and people are getting saved, we should carry on. Maybe a look at the apostle Paul's movements would be helpful. Sometimes he would only stay a few days in places, sometimes weeks, other places months, and in some places years. It would be clear that he was neither tied to a diary nor a committee. God helped us in Ballymagarrick and a nice number got saved. Some who were long prayed for were gathered in.

After a short break we commenced in Ardmore, on the Lough Neagh shore where there was a nice active, if small assembly. As the Christians were highly respected it was comparatively easy to get the neighbours in. Over years of gospel work we have learned that the general public is not much concerned about doctrinal beliefs etc, but they do watch the lives of those who profess to be Christians. It is nice to be able to mention the names of the saints and to hear them well spoken of by their neighbours. This was our experience at Ardmore, as it has been in many other places. God gave us a few souls and we enjoyed our stay there.

Our brother Mr Gilbert Stewart, who lived in Cork and labours in the Irish Republic, asked me to have some meetings in the assembly hall in Cork city. I was happy to do so and try to be of help to the small assembly in that large, dark city. The other assemblies in that area, Bandon and Skibbereen, gave us a good measure of support, our numbers were fairly good and God gave some blessing in salvation.

After Cork Mr McKelvey and I had ministry for a week in Ardmore, Mullafernaghan (when one got saved), Ahoghill and Ballymagarrick. When we see some saved at gospel meetings we like to visit later and if possible guide them in 'paths of righteousness'.

In 1969, towards the end of the summer, our country had serious troubles which have continued for many years, with much destruction of property and loss of life. The assembly at Oldpark Road, Belfast, though very near to these troubled areas thought they would like to have a gospel effort, so Mr McKelvey and I went to them. We were not interfered with in any way, but it was difficult even for members of the assembly, as some lived where they had to cross a 'peace line' before 9.00 pm. We did our best, but made no progress. Sad to say the assembly is no longer in existence and the nice hall has been sold.

The winter of 1969 saw me in Ballymena again where there have been a number of fruitful efforts. On this visit I was joined by brother Mr R Beattie. This proved to be a very happy and profitable time when quite a number professed conversion and the believers were uplifted.

A farmer at Carncullagh who had a portable hall in his yard had enquired several times about the possibility of a gospel effort there. Mr McKelvey had a long association with the area and was concerned about several young men who were connected with the believers but not saved. So he and I joined and God rewarded the exercise. We had the joy of seeing several young men saved who are now leaders in the local assembly. The weather was bitterly cold and the hall 'not completely draught proof', but God's presence and the warmth of the Christians made up for any other problems. That hall has been replaced and a good Sunday school and monthly gospel meeting continues there.

After these meetings in that northern part I went to Skibbereen, the most southerly town in Ireland, where I have enjoyed visits in gospel and ministry. The saints are well taught, steady and wise in assembly matters. They seek to keep gospel activity going and from time to time God works among them as He did on this visit.

For quite some time I had thought a united effort in Belfast would be good. I asked for an opportunity to speak with the overseeing brethren in the city assemblies when they met to discuss arrangements for the annual Easter Conference. I told them what I was thinking of and was thankful when they expressed their pleasure at such an idea, and assured me of their fellowship and support. I had hoped to have a local evangelist to join me in the meetings but it didn't work out that way. Quite a number of local brethren rallied around and helped with advertising, invitations, leaflets (covering much of the city), acting as stewards getting the people seated, and several who lead the singing in their assembly meetings came and sat on the platform along with other overseers. We arranged tables at the rear of the Ulster Hall for tracts, gospel booklets etc. Many availed themselves of the free offer of all this gospel material. On the first night we had almost 1300 in attendance, and on our closing meeting around 1600 — the place was packed. God preserved our meetings from disturbance or interference of any kind and was pleased to grant us His presence and help, and quite a number we know of professed salvation. When making the original plans, I accepted responsibility for all the costs of hiring the building etc, but when finished, all was paid for and some over. I'll admit it was quite a responsibility for me as I felt the strain and many a night tension marked me, but I proved God's enabling grace.

When right after those meetings in the Ulster Hall Mr McKelvey and I went to Clough, Co Antrim, it was quite a change. A small assembly and not large meetings, but I was as happy there as in the Ulster Hall. We learn over the years that numbers are not the most important thing as God can and does work in both small and large meetings. He gave us to see souls saved in Clough. The village is called 'Cold Clough' but amongst the Christians the fellowship was warm and most happy.

After Clough we had tent meetings in Cullybackey in association with the Ballywatermoy assembly. As far as I know only one professed, a small boy, but he is now a married man and an acceptable preacher of the gospel. He and his father shared the gospel meeting in our own assembly some weeks ago. Quite unexpectedly, my wife had far-out relatives from New Zealand who came to visit on Sunday afternoon. She invited them to the meeting. She was delighted they were in and said, "it was one of the best gospel meetings for some time".

The assembly in Plantation Street, Glasgow, had erected a hall at Harley Street, Ibrox, in 1971 and invited me for gospel meetings. They were good workers and kept up virile gospel testimony. I was pleased to join with them in 'holding forth the word of life'. A colony of what is called the 'Wee Frees', a group of people of Presbyterian thinking live in the area. In some way they became interested in our meetings, quite a number of them came and some got saved. I had arranged to be in another place later, but such was the interest, we could not close the meetings and so the others had to be put off. The hall was full nightly with a variety of people, Scottish, Irish, English. Pakistanis. In all, almost twenty professed salvation. Some of the 'Wee Frees' asked if I would go to the island of Lewis where they had relations. I appreciated the invitation, but was not free to go.

Back in Ireland I commenced in Ballywalter. The assembly had passed through a number of trying times. The leading brother in the assembly rang me and, telling me of changes of different kinds, almost begged me to help if I could. I responded and God blessed their exercise and a nice season of blessing resulted. That dear brother has since been called home, but God has raised up others and the assembly, while small, carries on steadily.

Ballywatermoy assembly asked for some Bible readings and ministry, a week of each. Mr McKelvey and I went. We took up some chapters in 1 Corinthians and in ministry what we felt would be of help to them. This was followed by ministry meetings in Kingsbridge (Belfast) and Annalong.

I had an aunt whose sister and family lived in Boston, Mass, USA. She was anxious to go and visit them, but never having been in a plane, she said she would only go if I would go with her and she would pay all the expenses. I could take her to the family, leave her there for a few weeks, and bring her home again. I did this, made a few visits, and had meetings in Boston, Philadelphia, Toronto and New York. When it was first suggested my wife said, "Don't make too firm arrangements for meetings, I can't see your aunt on a plane," but all went smoothly and my aunt throughly enjoyed the plane and the visit and so did I.

Coming back I had conference meetings at Redditch, Birmingham and Blackburn, Lancs, after which Mr Beattie and I had good gospel meetings in Cookstown with some getting saved. Then another visit to Skibbereen and still a further encouragement in salvation. A further gospel series in Rasharkin by Mr McKelvey and myself proved fruitful in salvation.

At that time I was stricken with diabetes and was out of active gospel work for some months. When I recovered somewhat, Mr McKelvey and I went to Banbridge. I have happy memories of Banbridge. I was saved, baptised and married there and often think of counsel, guidance and encouragement I received when I was first received into the assembly and throughout the years. Our gospel meetings were large and encouraging and several professed to be saved and have given us joy as they have continued happily in the ways of the Lord. Lungs, an assembly in the Clogher valley was formed after fruitful meetings that Mr T Campbell and Mr S Wright held and God has worked there over the years. They invited us in the winter of 1972, and while our meetings were not very large, unsaved people came and God wrought in salvation. While older men, who were leaders have been called home, God has raised up others to carry on. The assembly now meets in a nice new hall.

Glengormley of recent years has become a large and busy area on the outskirts of Belfast. The assembly has also grown and is active in gospel work amongst young and old. Mr McKelvey and I were invited for a gospel effort which we were very happy to engage in. God helped and people were saved.

The only time we had our meetings upset during the years of trouble in the province was when we were in Dungannon. In 1973 the assembly had hired a local school building, thinking people might come better there than to the gospel hall. The meetings had started and were shaping nicely and two had professed. One evening while we were sitting at tea in a Christian's home, there was a loud explosion. The bomb was not intended for the hall we were in but it was damaged. The streets around were littered with broken glass and rubble. When we went down to see how things were, the police officer said, "I can have the street cleared for you, but I am not sure as to other bombs, there may be more." Mr McKelvey, who by nature was of a rather careful disposition, when he saw it said, "Jim, I think I will quietly slip home to Ballymena, you can finish off without me". This I did and the effort was over.

The assembly in Larne had erected a lovely new hall at Curran Road. We were asked for the opening meetings. Mr McKelvey had a sister living in Larne and he was interested in her salvation — she was not young anymore. She attended the meetings, and with others, professed to be saved. Not long after the meetings she passed away, but had lived long enough to show the reality of her profession.

I have had a life-long interest in the Lessans assembly. My mother in early life was in fellowship there; in 1917 my father was commended to the work of the Lord from that assembly and it has been a joy to me to have several efforts in the gospel with them. In 1973 Mr McKelvey and I had fruitful meetings there, and in 1996 Mr S Thompson and I had two short series. The numbers were most encouraging and once again, God blessed in salvation.

After Mr McKelvey and I were in Lessans we went to Ballylintagh in Co Londonderry. For some years the assembly was small and weak. A sister whose husband was in fellowship there sought to help and encourage as best she could in a sister's sphere. Her doctor, a young man who was saved and interested in spiritual matters, had long and serious talks with her about his position and that of the assembly, with the result that he and his wife came into the assembly. He proved to be a real help in the spread of the gospel. The doctor to whom I refer passed away very suddenly after a heart attack. His wife and family continue in happy fellowship. One of his sons gave up a good business, and with his young wife and children went to labour in the gospel in Norway. They are seeing some interest and with work amongst young and old, the gospel is being made known in that spiritually dark and materialistic country. The doctor, with others, saw a nice hall erected to which we went for meetings. God set the seal of His approval upon their work and a nice number professed conversion.

We had gospel meetings in Harryville assembly, Ballymena, Mr McKelvey's home assembly. For some reason I have always found Ballymena to be fruitful in the gospel. In all, I have had eight special efforts there and in each of them God worked in Salvation. At the series in Harryville at least 13 professed salvation and the saints were encouraged. When I was first in Ballymena in 1949, there was no assembly in Harryville, just a good Sunday School and gospel outreach. Since the assembly was formed it has grown and they now have a good hall and have had the joy of seeing God working with them.

We had an intererst in some in the Carncullagh area and arranged meetings there. While our meetings were not large, God visited with help and blessing, a number professing salvation. We had some ministry meetings after that in Ballylintagh, Harryville, Straidarren, Kingsmoss and Ballycastle.

Lurgan is a well known centre and the assembly there invited us for gospel meetings, which we commenced in May 1975. For many years their annual conference and Bible readings have been very well attended and made a blessing to many. The assembly of late years purchased a new and large hall, giving them the facilities for catering and accommodating large numbers. However the meetings we had were in the old hall. We had good numbers and interest, God giving us to see a number saved and the saints encouraged.

In 1975 I was invited to Norway to help in their conference meetings and in these I joined with our esteemed brother Mr A Leckie. Not being able to speak Norwegian we had to use an interpreter. It was Mr Leckie's first time to speak in that way, I had done it several times before. Mr Leckie spoke first and finished in about 15-20 minutes. After the meeting he said to me, "Jim, that's hopeless", but he soon got used to it and gave the saints helpful and upbuilding ministry. Numbers were quite good, and as well as assembly members we had Christians from churches etc. I was back in the area again in 1981 in association with the assemblies in Norway and Denmark. For many years it would seem many of these countries had little in the way of active gospel work, although in earlier years God blessed the labours of men like Mr James Lees, Mr A McGregor and others. It is good to know that recent years have seen some being commended to these parts, and it is good to know of their earnest labours. I had a short series of gospel meetings in Esbjerg where Mr D Saunders and his wife, with Mr & Mrs McCullagh live, both couples are from Northern Ireland. While engaged in secular work, they carry on in gospel work and God has blessed their labours and a nice assembly has been brought into being, but vast areas and great numbers of people 'sit in darkness'.

Buckna was our next place for gospel meetings. Mr McKelvey was concerned about a number of young men whose parents were in assembly fellowship. We had the joy of seeing God work amongst them and a good number professed to be saved and have gone on to bring joy and to be of help in assembly life and testimony.

After Buckna we were in Kingsmoss where again God worked and some were saved. The Lungs assembly, where many gospel efforts were conducted, had an interest in the village of Brookeborough and asked if I would be interested to have some meetings there in a portable hall. I asked Mr Aiken who recently had been commended to full-time service if he would join me, which he did. He was detained elsewhere for two weeks before he joined me. A local brother with a sense of humour, when the meetings had started said, "Art thou he that should come, or look we for another?" It was a most happy time, numbers were good, and God's presence and help were felt. We saw a nice number of cases of conversion, and it was clear we were both in the will of God. After that series Mr McKelvey and I had meetings in Magherafelt with a little interest, and then Gransha, where the meetings were disappointing. Later in Ballywatermoy, we saw good numbers and had blessing in salvation. In Lisburn we again saw the hand of God and rejoiced in God's blessing. The small struggling assembly in Cork City asked for some gospel meetings. For many years they have maintained a witness in the large Roman Catholic city. In earlier years the assembly was quite large, but when I was there in 1976 it was small. When preaching, I like meetings to start and finish on time. A large grocery chain in Northern Ireland announces 'open from eight till late' and it would seem some preachers are like that! In Cork I couldn't get the meetings started on time, the people were just not there, but then after the meeting they would sit around and talk. They seem to 'count not time by years', however God gave us good interest and numbers and granted His help and blessing. One boy who was saved then has grown up and matured in divine things and is a real help in other parts of Ireland.

Drum, Co Monaghan, is another place where of late years,

the assembly has become small. They have been very active in the gospel in many ways and while they get good numbers of local people they have not seen much fruit in salvation. Mr Aiken and I have had two series there and greatly enjoyed the warm, hearty fellowship of the saints. They still carry on their annual conference and get the hall packed. God seems in a special way to help in this meeting.

Early in January 1977 Mr McKelvey and I spent some time in the USA and Canada, a gospel effort in Bryn Mawr, where some were saved, and then conference and ministry meetings. We both had many friends there and appreciated their invitations and hospitality. They seemed encouraged and helped in the ministry meetings.

The assemblies in Lancashire, England, operate a very good gospel tent work and it has been my privilege to have gospel meetings with them on a number of occasions. In June of 1977 I was in Rishton, Lancs. Mr D McMaster, an evangelist from Scotland, joined me. He preached to the children, and I was responsible for the adult meetings. The site for the meetings was granted by the Roman Catholic priest, and a very good place

Rishton, Lancs, 1983: D A McMaster, J G Hutchinson.

it was. We had interesting and profitable meetings, and several professed conversion. Children from a family came and their father was encouraged to come. He was a terrorist who had fled his home and was living near the tent. We had long and interesting talks with him. We must leave the results with a wise and gracious God.

After Manchester we had tent meetings in Ballynahinch, where in earlier times I had a fruitful spell in the gospel hall. The weather on the whole was favourable, we found the local people easy to visit and quite a number attended. A man from Lisburn, recently saved, brought his wife and family each night and his wife got saved, as well as some others.

The Frances Street assembly in Newtownards have for many years run a monthly meeting for the ladies of the district, with a gospel message and a cup of tea. It was arranged that I should have a week with them each evening. The numbers were very encouraging and at least one dear lady got saved. The principal of a local school came, a lady not accustomed to gospel meetings, she seemed to show some interest.

The assembly at Wellington Street, Ballymena, had erected a fine hall on Cambridge Avenue and asked for a series of meetings. The assembly rallied around the effort and we were helped. In the first few nights two young men got saved, and in the weeks we were there quite a number of others professed and give us joy as they mature in the things of God. Some thought the meetings should continue, but I had promised to join Mr R Jordan in Dundonald. Meetings in Dundonald and Dromore followed the Ballymena effort. Both were difficult and small, but the "seed was sown" and we do well to keep in mind "the harvest is the end of the age", not the end of the meetings!

After the Dromore meetings, some suggested a tent effort a little way out of Dromore. I mentioned this to Mr McKelvey but he was not keen. Years were creeping on and he felt tent work too strenuous. I asked Mr J Allen who was home from Malaysia if he would be interested and he was. Together we commenced what proved to be a very fruitful spell of meetings. Some in whom we had an interest in Dromore attended and got saved. A mother who had a son not saved travelled fifty miles each night and towards the end of the meetings, he got saved. Talking to him after he was saved, he said, "The word 'believing' puzzled me" but now he said, "I have got a better word, I am like Abraham, I am fully persuaded". He has gone on to study the Scriptures and to be of help amongst the believers in various places.

The saints in South Wales wished another visit. Over the years I have been with them quite a lot. The assembly in Llanelli has been large and greatly blessed on many occasions, and this time was no exception. We had well attended meetings and some blessing in salvation. While there I had a week of ministry with the assembly at Bynea, where I had laboured earlier.

Later in that year I had a further visit to Skibbereen where the faithful little assembly encourages the gospel in their area. While they may not see great movements quite regularly some get saved and added to the company. The light of the gospel shines brightly in that needy part of the Irish Republic.

At the beginning of 1979 Mr McKelvey and I were in Comber. We were encouraged right from the start with a sense of God's presence and excellent attendance. Some got saved and today are in Comber, Ballygigan, and Dundonald assemblies. We often find when neighbouring assemblies take an interest and support the gospel efforts, they share the blessing and see their numbers increased. It was so at that series. It seems a pity that in some instances people are interested only in their own place — 'ourselves alone'.

Our next gospel effort was in Kingsmills, Co Tyrone. Aughavey and Kingsmills assemblies have worked closely together for many years, almost 'twin assemblies'. In going there I had happy reminders of my first visit to Aughavey in 1946, some saved then were in Kingsmills and joined heartily with us in the effort. Numbers were fairly good and some professed salvation who have gone on and given us joy to see their spiritual progress. The assembly, one of the early assemblies in Northern Ireland, had later erected a lovely new hall and were having a few special opening meetings. They asked Mr McKelvey and me if we would be responsible to speak. These were very happy nights. People from the town and district came in to hear the gospel and as well to see the building. Christians from around the area came to enjoy the ministry and encourage the assembly.

I was invited for a week of ministry in Teignmouth, Devon,

and in Manchester, after which we were in Antrim for gospel meetings. Since the new hall was opened there the assembly has grown and their gospel meetings have been encouraging. For the series at this time, we had good numbers and interest with quite a few professing salvation. We moved from Antrim to Broughshane where again, in the goodness of God, we saw a further move and people getting saved. In writing one hesitates to say much regarding God's working, lest it should appear as if we were 'boasting'. For if blessing comes it must be from God and it is well to record His doing and ascribe all the praise to Him.

A young woman from Co Carlow got saved with her husband in Co Down. She was concerned about her parents and family and asked if anything could be done in the way of meetings in their area. Mr A Aiken and I borrowed a mobile hall from Mr G Stewart, and getting ground we placed it not too far from where the folks we were interested in lived. Then we went to look for lodgings. There were no assembly Christians within many miles of where we were and so a couple of saved people, Church of Ireland, asked where we were to stay? We said, "We don't know", to which they replied, "If you were to stay with us, would that suit you?" We happily arranged with them. Their house, an old farmhouse lacking in modern amenities, was about half a mile from the hall but we had a really happy month with them and appreciated their kindness and care. It was a joy to visit daily and talk to the people and leave gospel literature. Numbers at the meetings were good and one elderly lady got saved. We left the area feeling satisfied that the gospel was made known in that dark county.

We came up north and with Mr McKelvey commenced in the gospel at Lungs. The assembly was concerned about some of the young people connected with the believers. God rewarded their exercise in the salvation of some of these who have gone on well in spiritual things.

In Bandon in Co Cork there is a long established assembly in this fairly Protestant town. It was blessed in earlier years with having good leaders and men who were deeply interested in the spread of the gospel. Earlier, I had had fruitful gospel meetings and in 1980 was invited for another effort. I found their numbers in fellowship had considerably decreased and it was not easy to get the local people in to the meetings. some came and we leave the results with God.

Cloughfern is one of the assemblies established in more recent years. Saints associated with Fortwilliam assembly had an interest in children's work in that district for a number of years and as the work grew and developed the assembly was formed in happy fellowship with the neighbouring meetings. Mr McKelvey and I were invited for an effort in the gospel. We found quite an interest and had well attended meetings at which some got saved and have gone on to give joy to the assembly and ourselves. Cloughfern carries on a Saturday night ministry meeting and endeavours to get speakers to guide, instruct and feed the saints. It has been my privilege to be there quite often.

In the summer of 1980 Mr G Stewart and I had tent meetings at Killinchy, where in earlier years Mr McKelvey and I had large and very fruitful meetings. There used to be an assembly at Ardmillan close by, but it has been closed for several years. Gilbert and I enjoyed the visitations and the meetings and while nice numbers came, we heard of no-one getting saved.

For several years Mullafernaghan has had seasons of blessing. It would seem that for some time all is quiet despite gospel activity, then things move and they see blessing. November, December of 1980 was one of these times when Mr J Allen and I were there. The hall was full each night and God worked in grace and quite a number professed salvation. Mr J Stewart and my father had an experience there like that in 1919. Later Mr Stewart and Mr Wallace and later still Mr E Wishart and Mr S Thompson saw God working there. It is something we cannot explain, why sometimes districts see this and others do not.

In 1981 Mr McKelvey and I were in Clonkeen. It was to him "an old hunting ground", it was my first time there. Meetings were well attended and some were saved. Of late years God has prospered His work in relation to this assembly.

For several weeks we, in some respects like the apostles, "visted our brethren...where we had preached the word", in Gransha, Skibbereen, Kingsbridge, Letterkenny, Killycurragh, Bangor (Central Hall), Castlereagh and Kingsmoss. We had a few meetings, and we found there was an increasing demand for such visits. God's people felt they needed help.

I had an invitation to Denmark for their annual conference

meetings, when saints from Norway, Sweeden, and the Faroe Islands gathered with the Danish saints. The week of Bible readings, ministry meetings and the gospel was intensive, but most enjoyable.

Coming back, Mr Jim Allen and I tried gospel meetings in a tent at Markethill. The interest was reasonably good and local people responded favourably with blessing in salvation. At the end of that summer I was at Irvine, Scotland, for their annual conference and a week's ministry, followed by the conference at Chapelhall and a further week of ministry. I was beginning to feel I would need to be careful and not get taken up with ministry to the neglect of the gospel, to which I was satisfied God had called me.

I had had several communications from the assembly at Northfield, Birmingham, and they were anxious I should go for a gospel effort, which I did in September 1981. I found the assembly warm-hearted, active and desiring to go on in the ways of God. They had a good contact with the local people and were highly respected in the area. The numbers were quite good and several professed salvation. I left the assembly happy, thankful for God's help and blessing.

Right after this Mr McKelvey and I went to Annalong with the gospel. I had been there in previous efforts — this one was the most fruitful. We had the interest and support of local assemblies and it pleased God to work. A nice number professed salvation and the assembly was encouraged and helped.

Ahoghill, in County Antrim, where I first had meetings with my father in 1948, was our next port of call. Again we enjoyed the presence and help of God and saw His hand at work. The assembly there has been a testimony for God for many years. While old and respected leaders have been called home, God has raised up others and the work goes on. In recent years, it was decided to change the conference date from Christmas Day to 1st January. This has proved to be a wise decision as the conference has grown in size and it continues to be a season of blessing.

We went to Ballyclare after that, where again we saw the hand of God, some professing salvation and a nice local interest. About this time, I was beginning to notice a changing attitude in both saint and sinner. There was not the burden and concern in the saints (I am not referring to Ballyclare at all) nor the interest of local people in divine matters. Over all the years it has been going that way, sad to say. It is likely an indication of the last days.

Mr John Flynn had been going to Egypt for various meetings. With the co-operation of the assemblies there, he invited me to join him for a month for their conference meetings and gospel in 1982. We flew by Hungarian Airlines as they were offering the best rates. Calling in at Budapest, we spent a night there and had a meeting with the believers. The assemblies there seemed to be getting on fairly well despite restrictions etc. Arriving at Cairo airport we were warmly welcomed by assembly leaders. Believing as they do in 2 Corinthians 13:12, and not at all using electric shavers or aftershave, it was a 'different reception', but they were kind, good and appreciative. I was to stay in an apartment above a doctor's surgery, and his wife sent me up my food. In the country, generally "litter free and strict hygiene" were not top priorities, but we kept busy the whole month. The conference meetings were held in a large building in a central location and were well attended. One of the local evangelists (there were five at that time) accompanied me, and knowing English, was able to interpret for me. He was a humble, devout little man who had the glory of God and the blessing of others in view.

An English businessman with a real interest in the welfare of the work in that land, so often mentioned in Holy Scripture, joined in sharing the ministry. At that time there were 22 asemblies, others have commenced since then, and despite severe restrictions the work of the assemblies has prospered. At the various meetings several professed conversion and quite a number who had been saved earlier were baptised. I found in the various assemblies godly women and well taught leaders. Some of the older folk remembered with affection Mr John Moneypenny who had a daughter teaching there, and for several years he was detained in the country in wartime conditions. In earlier years, Mr J W Clapham and Mr G Knowles and others did much to open up the country to the gospel and establish assemblies. I have sought to keep in touch a little and have arranged for suitable magazines and literature to be sent, but at times, owing to strict censorship, some of it may not get

Speaking in Egypt; Mr B Arteen interpreting.

With some of the workers in Egypt.

to the folk concerned. Because of my diabetic condition the food did not suit me too well. In a month I lost 14 pounds weight. Some might like to, or would need to, go! At almost the end of the visit, being in the centre of Cairo, I saw a large English hotel. I said to John Flynn, "I am going in there, and whatever it costs me, I'll have some good English tea". We did, and the tea was first class, and the price reasonable. Only once in all the years did my wife say, "I would rather you didn't go". This was when I had invitations for further meetings in Egypt.

When I returned home Mr McKelvey and I started gospel meetings in the Straid school, Ballymena. Some of the believers had refurbished the old school house and made it suitable and comfortable for the meetings. We had loyal support from the Christians in the area and quite a number of unsaved people came to hear the gospel. We had joy and liberty in preaching, and there were 'signs following' with several professing salvation.

After that we were in Killycurragh for further gospel meetings. The assembly came into being in the days of Mr Andrew Frazer, a godly schoolmaster, who gave up his secular post to engage in the work of the Lord. His health was not good, and later he went to live in California, where he was a great blessing among the saints and in the gospel. His physical condition worsened and at a comparatively early age, God called him home. Our meetings in Killycurragh were only fair. We enjoyed the whole-hearted fellowship of the assembly, but could not speak of results in the gospel.

For some reason Mr McKelvey was not keen to have meetings in Belfast, but when Castlereagh assembly invited us, he was persuaded to go. It turned out to be a season of rich blessing. In days when city assemblies were finding it difficult to get the neighbours in, Castlereagh got excellent numbers, due perhaps to the constant visitations of the local brethren. God blessed His Word and a good number got saved.

In 1983 the Aberdeen assemblies invited Mr J Allen and myself for their annual Bible Readings and Ministry Meetings. The Bible readings were not large, but I thought them happy and profitable. The ministry meetings in the evening were large and God gave His presence. Before returning, we had visits to Cullen, Peterhead and Buckie.

At home again we were quickly into the gospel. This time in a portable hall on the outskirts of Newry. On other visits Mr McKelvey and I had fruitful meetings, not this time as meetings were small and not encouraging.

My wife and I were invited for a holiday in Jersey, a delightful place, but when you go there for a few days they expect you to take the assembly meetings! The assembly meets in a lovely hall, and has above it a very good apartment used for missionaries and visiting evangelists etc. Many of the Lord's servants find rest and refreshment there. Gospel-wise, it would seem little progress is made. A pleasure-loving and affluent people, they seem to have little concern regarding eternal things. Nevertheless, the gospel is preached.

I was invited for further meetings in Rishton, Lancashire, where the assembly is very weak and small. We would fear for it's future. The Lancs. gospel tent was the venue for the meetings. Mr D McMaster was responsible for the Children's work, my responsibility was with the adults and ministry. We had a good intererst and some professions of conversion.

Mr McKelvey's mother came from Ballywalter and a number of relations were still in the district, so when we were asked for meetings he was anxious to go. It proved to be his last gospel effort. In fact his last time to preach. We commenced on the Lord's Day and he seemed his usual self, though I thought I detected he was slowing up quite a bit. He was in his 88th year. On the second Wednesday night he went first and read the Scripture and started to preach. Sitting behind him I noticed him leaning to the right, but still quite clear in his preaching. In a few minutes he was leaning much more. I spoke to him and said, "Would it be better if you stood over behind the desk?" He said, "Jim, I cannot", and with that he collapsed, and I caught him. We placed him in a chair and carried him out. Taking him to where he was staying, the friends tried without success to get a doctor. The police were able to get an ambulance and he was taken to the Ards Hospital. He had had a severe stroke and for several days hovered between consciousness and unconsciousness. A nursing sister, whose relations were in a Co Londonderry assembly was, with others, very kind and attentive to him. She rang me one morning at about 2.00am and said, "Your old friend has gone down quite a bit. I think you should come". I did, and about 8.00am he passed away, as he lived, with dignity and peace. He had written out for me details of his funeral service and his wishes regarding the disposal of his belongings. I sought to carry these out exactly as he had wished. His funeral from the Harryville Gospel Hall was very large, the saints felt the loss of a dignified and honourable servant of God. I felt keenly the loss of a true fellow labourer. We had 18 years together, and I learned so much from him, and never an unkind word passed between us. It was a real joy to work with him. He was so agreeable and helpful. At his funeral I was responsible to speak in the hall and Mr J S Wallace at the grave.

I carried on the meetings in Ballywalter and God gave some interest and a few professed salvation. I then went to Strabane and God gave us to see two professing who have gone on well and given us joy.

Mr Aiken and I went to Holywood, Co Down, where a couple from Canada, home on holiday, were encouraged to attend. The husband had a background of Christian teaching while his wife, of German extraction, had none, she had never been to a Sunday school or gospel meetings. We had the joy of seeing them both saved and baptised before they returned to Canada where a short time later she was stricken with cancer and was called home. Other local people professed during the meetings.

I was again in Skibbereen and saw some further conversions. I stayed over for the Cork conference, which has grown to be a feature in that needy part, not only being well attended by assembly believers, but also quite a number of saints associated with the systems around come and are helped in the ways of God.

In 1984 the members of Laganvale assembly had interest in having a large tent pitched in Botanic Gardens and asked Mr J Allen and me to conduct the meetings. We had a very profitable month of gospel meetings, excellent attendance and God working in salvation. Just prior to these meetings I was with the assembly at Kilbarchan, Scotland, for their conference, also with the assembly at Rockhampton, Bristol, for their conference and a week of ministry. I also had some ministry meetings with the Merrion Hall assembly, Dublin. I had been going to them for many years and was sorry to see their numbers decreasing. When I was there first, they had at least 250 in fellowship and quite a large gospel meeting.

Botanic Gardens, 1984.

The small assembly at New Bradwell, England, had some Irish connections and wished me to visit them with the gospel. I did, and I am glad I did. I discerned a keen interest in the gospel and a desire for New Testament teaching. The Lord blessed the visit and several professed salvation. We see some of the converts now living in Ireland and showing indications of divine life.

Mr A Aiken and I had several weeks in Omagh in 1984, where God gave interest and blessing was seen in the gospel, several professing salvation. For many years Omagh has been blessed in many ways. Mr Rodgers lived there and gave much valuable teaching in that assembly and in the small assemblies in that area. Mr R Beattie spent all his married life in Omagh and was highly respected in the assembly and in the town. He was a kind, pleasant, at times jovial man, whose presence and preaching were a real influence for good.

We visited Ballymagarrick again and had several weeks of gospel meetings. During the meetings we had a snow storm. One night we had no light, no heat and very few people. It was thought best to have a short meeting which we had with the aid of tilley lamps. A ten-minute message was given, a familiar hymn sung, during which a young man got saved. We felt like one of old "who slew a lion in a pit on a snowy day"

The assembly at Fernielea, Aberdeen, invited me for a gospel series, with Mr G Forbes to take care of the children's work. We had happy and good meetings with some blessing in salvation.

After this I was in Kingsmoss and Derby, England. One professed in Derby and I hear has gone on well.

Mr J Allen was going to Malaysia for another visit, in 1985, and asked me to join him. A kind brother was responsible for my return flight. Malaysia was a new experience, but one greatly enjoyed. Mr Allen enjoys the confidence of the saints there, having lived and laboured amongst them for years, first in school teaching and later in full-time missionary work. We had interesting meetings en route in Singapore where we enjoyed the whole-hearted fellowship of a Chinese assembly, saints who love the Lord and His work and ways. We found the same in the Malaysian assemblies, Paramount assembly, Klang and Malacca. It was evident that God had been working and it was delightful to see so many young believers with a real hunger for the Word of God and a concern for the salvation of others. We enjoyed the presence and help of the Lord. Several professed to be saved. I was able in 1989 to pay a return visit as I was on my way to Australia. The warmth and kindness of the saints will be long remembered. There I was introduced to good Chinese food, which I got to like. I said to my fellow labourers that eating out was a national pastime! I have had several pressing invitations to return, but it is too late in the day, or so my family tell me! May others go to help. Irish brethren, McVey; Wilson; Allen and Bentley have given many years of service with the blessing of God.

Coming home from Malaysia Mr Allen and I had gospel meetings in Banbridge. It was nice to be back again where I was saved, baptised, received and married. It was a season of real interest and blessing when some long prayed for got saved and night by night the hall was filled. Two Roman Catholic men got saved and have given us much joy since. One has a hairdressing business in Newry. All around the shop are gospel texts and he talks to all his customers about the Saviour. Some religious

Gospel Meetings in Klang.

Malaysia.

leaders who were customers have ceased to be his clients, but God has given him many others.

The assembly in Moncton, NB, Canada, asked me for gospel meetings in September 1985. I was happy to go and be of what help I could. I didn't find the meetings easy, and no one I knew of got saved. I was very stirred on Lord's Day at the remembrance meeting, when an Indian brother, saved a very short time, gave out the hymn and emphasised the words, "And can it be that I should gain an interest in the Saviour's blood?' I thought, there he was away from that dark and distant land and appreciating the work of Christ, while so many favoured have no interest.

After Moncton I had some nights of ministry in Halifax, Boston, Cleveland, Chicago, Iowa, Calgary and Toronto. Before returning home I had a gospel effort in Marple assembly, PA, with Mr Gordon Reager. The assembly was small but warm-hearted and exercised about the large district around. God gave us to see a little blessing in salvation. It was arranged to have an open-air meeting in a large public square and I was asked to be the speaker. We had an excellent hearing. One enquirer, no doubt hearing an Irish accent, asked if I was associated with Bernadette Devlin, of civil rights fame!

Preparing for a farewell feast, Malaysia.
A custom in Malaysia when someone is going away.

Tent at Ballee, Ballymena, June-July 1986 J. Allen and J G Hutchinson.

Ritton House Sq., Philadelphia, August 1971.

Tent in Adelaide, Australia, Left to right;
Mr L Strahan, J G Hutchinson, Dr Pain

Just after that I was with the North Shields assembly for their Easter conference, sharing with Mr J Hunter and Mr J Dickson.

In 1986 the Cambridge Avenue assembly and the Harryville assembly in Ballymena united for a gospel series in a large 1000-seater tent. Mr Allen and I were asked to conduct the meetings. The number of local people that attended was most encouraging, local Christians and many from further away took an interest and the tent was full most nights. God answered prayer and a nice number got saved. It would seem a good measure of the spirit of the '59 revival still remains, some would speak of the area as the 'Bible Belt'.

Mr S Thompson was concerned about the area around Carryduff and arranged that he and I would have some meetings in a portable hall. The interest was not very good, but some came, and God gave a little blessing in salvation. Of later years the assembly there has a new hall and their numbers are increased. They have a good Sunday school and get a good Sunday evening meeting.

In 1970 I had a gospel effort in Bute Hall, Prestwick. At that time a coffee morning was commenced which continues to the time of writing. They get more unsaved neighbours to that meeting than to any other meeting. The assembly invited Mr Aiken and myself for a further spell in the gospel. We enjoyed the meetings. The attendances were good, and God gave a little blessing in Salvation. After Prestwick I was in Broomhedge again with Mr Aiken. It was nice to see some who were saved at tent meetings there in 1953 still there and going on well. We had fair numbers, but not a lot of interest. We did not hear of any getting saved. At that year I was back at Harley Street, Glasgow, for the conference meetings. To me these seasons were times of refreshing and help.

After Glasgow I was in Blackburn, Lancs, for their conference meetings. This was another area of gospel work in previous years. While I was there, I was called home for two funerals, calls which I could not refuse. Both of the deceased were very good friends of mine. I have always felt I should give funerals priority, when at such times hearts are heavy and need comfort and help.

Ballyduff assembly on the outskirts of Belfast is an assembly of recent origin. Believers from neighbouring assemblies had given much time and effort to children's work in the district. They also tried gospel meetings, local brethren giving much help. Mr J Campbell and Mr J Hay from Scotland were brought over for meetings and worked diligently for some weeks. God blessed the work of the saints, and soon a small assembly was started with the full fellowship of the other assemblies nearby. A good hall was erected, much of which was due to the interest and generosity of a local building contractor. The assembly took a real interest in the people of the large estate, visiting the sick, bringing presents when a child was born, sending flowers and attending funerals. In every way they show themselves interested in the blessing of the people. This was one of the reasons they got the people to come to the meetings. I have often thought about the words regarding the Lord Jesus, "He went about doing good". Not just abstaining from evil. We do not go in for the sins and pleasures of the world, and that is right, but what are we doing?

Mr Robert Revie and I were invited for a gospel series. Mr Revie was a missionary in Ethiopia, whose wife was saved at meetings in Annbank when Mr Jordan and I had the Ayrshire tent there. We saw good interest and numbers, and several professed to be saved.

After some further gospel meetings in Ballynahinch with Mr Allen, where there was very little interest, we had both been invited for a tent series in the city of Adelaide, Australia, the first tent meetings in the city for 50 years. We had a month there, much longer than the Australian assemblies are used to. The tent we used, a very good one, was loaned to us by Mr L Strahan. He came from the East of Australia and erected it for us in a lovely public park where the local Christians had obtained permission for it to be. The meetings were good and were supported by the local saints. God gave help, and several professed to be saved. I left Adelaide feeling that if there were some to launch out and concentrate on the gospel, something could be done. In fact, the last time I came home I said, "If I was 25 years younger, I would go back and spend some time in the gospel." But we cannot turn the clock back. It may be that some reading this with youth on their side may push out from the shore.

After Adelaide I was in Bayswater assembly in Melbourne for

gospel meetings, which I greatly enjoyed. The assembly was most active and hired a public hall to which many came and some hearing the word of life, believed and were saved.

In January 1987 I was joined by Mr R Eadie in Shanaghan. The Christians could say in the words of Holy Scripture "they are set on a hill", and truly from them, the light shines into the countryside. My father had the joy of the opening meetings in the hall they now occupy. God gave them at that time a season of real blessing and many times since as well. For us, in January — February, it was a happy and fruitful time. Some that we were interested in for years got saved, and a number of others as well. The assembly there goes along steadily, carrying on a good gospel work among young and old, and a good annual conference. After Shanaghan Mr Aiken and I were in the assembly at Ballykeel (Mourne), a nice assembly meeting in a good hall, not far from where "the Mountains of Mourne sweep down to the sea". We enjoyed visiting the district, where the assembly believers are esteemed. The people of the area are a warm-hearted and friendly people, though someone has said they have a good deal of the solidity of the granite around them. If they decide to do something, they are hard to change! We had good numbers and some got saved, A little later we were back for some ministry meetings to try and help the young in Christ. Mr J Allen and I joined in Bloomfield for a series in the gospel. While some professed it was not a very stirring time. The area was visited and much gospel literature was given out, and the gospel preached. "We know not what shall prosper".

Mr Aiken and I accepted another invitation to Harley Street, Glasgow, Another place of happy memories. Like most other areas it was difficult to get local folk in, yet we had quite good meetings with blessing in salvation. It will be noticeable to the observant that when God works and blesses the assembly, the Devil begins to work, and if possible mar what is of God. I thought I could see signs of unrest, not the sweet harmony and unity that once was there. In nearly all assembly problems I have known, very few have to do with truth or doctrine. All the more reason for troubles being solved and harmony restored. As long as two men are alive, there will be slight difference of opinions, but all this could be fixed with humility of mind and grace. It would be a great mercy if brethren on ALL sides would stop and ask, "Is Satan trying to use us in upsetting the love, peace and joy of the assembly?"

Waringstown assembly had asked Mr Allen and me for a series of tent meeetings in their village. The village has grown in recent times, but not their assembly, their numbers have decreased. We found those that were there hearty and unitedly behind the tent meetings. We had a little support from neighbouring assemblies, and quite a good local support. Some professed to be saved, and many others heard the way of life.

Later that year, I was in Fortwilliam assembly in Belfast. It is sad to see how many of the city assemblies have become small, and the generally poor response among the people around. I have noticed in recent years, especially in the city, that there is not the support from surrounding assemblies that there once was. Earlier, if there had been an effort in one assembly, many believers and their families would have regularly attended, not so now. I know many have their mid-week meetings, children's meetings etc, and there is a good deal of pressure on all. I see country assemblies doing much better in this way. We had fair attendance and the weekly 'friendship meetings' were very good. They, like other places, get more unsaved at this meeting. It was difficult to get them into other meetings.

For a third time I returned to Carncullagh, and was joined by Mr Aiken. The hall there is in the yard of Mr D McConaghy's farm. A good Sunday School is carried on in it, and a monthly gospel meeting. All this is in happy fellowship with the Ballycastle assembly. We had happy, fruitful weeks there with blessing in salvation. After this I was in Bandon and Skibbereen, for ministry and then over to New Stevenston, Scotland, for their annual conference. Quite unexpectedly in 1989 I received an invitation to Japan. Mr Currie wrote on behalf of the assemblies to see if I would go for some weeks, mainly for ministry. Having had several invitations to Vancouver, which I was unable to respond to, I thought it might be an opportunity to fit them in, and I arranged to go. On the way out I took in Boston, Philadelphia, Cleveland and Chicago. It was good to see the believers and renew happy fellowship. The Vancouver conference was most enjoyable. I was privileged to share the Bible readings and ministry with Mr R McPheat and Mr J R Baker. Together we sought to give help in a number of

Speaking in Japan. Mr J Currie interpreting.

Japan, some believers.

Chop sticks! Malaysia.

Vancouver assemblies. I then went on and flew from San Fransisco to Tokyo. Mr Currie and his good wife met me, and for the weeks very kindly and carefully looked after me. It was quite an experience, a new culture, another language, and apart from the Curries I was a complete stranger. The work of the assemblies has prospered there over the years. From two small assemblies when Mr Hay and Mr Wright went, the number has now grown to over one hundred. I was privileged to be with fourteen of these assemblies, and to have ministry and gospel meetings with them. Mr Currie accompanied me and was my interpreter, save one meeting, at which Mr R Cairns did this for me. It was nice to see the simple order of the gatherings and the interest of the local believers. I met with some of the Japanese evangelists and received kindness in their homes. I was happy to be at the conference at Yokohama, and shared the ministry with some of the local speakers. One could only feel thankful to see the earnest labours of the servants of the Lord and how God blessed their work. It was stirring to see the vast numbers of people at the railway stations, a moving mass of people. Being a little taller than the people in general, I stood and looked over their heads, a hard-working materialistic nation, wholly given to work and idol worship. I saw a little of the country but was not there for sightseeing. In measure, I felt like Paul in Acts 17:16, "His spirit was stirred in him". The good work of the bookshop was carried on by Miss Speechly and Miss Riddles. Mr Wright had started this in a small way many years earlier.

When returning from Japan I was in Malaysia for two weeks, and almost a week in Singapore. Such a visit to the Far East gives one an idea of the vast need, and one is challenged to think how few there are to preach the gospel.

Coming home I joined with Mr Allen in tent meetings associated with the Ahorey assembly. The tent was pitched near a small lake, where many gather on Sunday afternoons. The assembly conduct open-air meetings there and get a very good hearing. The weather was glorious, and conducive to good numbers. God blessed His Word, and some were saved. I was again in Holywood and later with the assembly in York Street, Leicester, for their annual weekend conference. I also visited Northfield, Birmingham, where earlier I had gospel meetings with blessing, and had a short visit to Broadways, Worcestershire, and Kempston, Bedford.

The assembly at Antrim desired another gospel effort. I asked Mr J S Wallace to join me, which he did. We had really good meetings, with a sense of God's presence and blessing. The hall was well filled each night and God worked in salvation. Almost immediately thereafter I joined Mr R Eadie in Newry. It was an unforgettable time. We commenced in early November and continued right over the Christmas season closing the meetings at the end of February. God really worked and quite a number got saved, some very interesting cases, some who have turned out to be of real help in the work of the assemblies, not only in Newry but in neighbouring assemblies also. I finished in Newry, and in two days I was off to Australia. When I phoned my wife from London before I got the plane for Australia, she told me of a young woman who had phoned our home to tell of getting saved in the early hours of that morning. I happened to remember the girl's number and had time to call her. She was able to tell of getting saved. I was very glad to hear that news as she had been very concerned and I felt sorry to think I was going to leave her that way.

My first meetings on arrival were in association with the

Bayswater assembly in Melbourne. The Lord rewarded the earnest and diligent work of the saints there, and some were saved. Some of the Christians had contacted an Irish Roman Catholic family and got them to attend. One of the young ladies got saved soon after the meetings, and with her husband are now in assembly fellowship. I have been able to visit with her parents in a southern Irish town, and though her parents are strict and devout Roman Catholics, they received me and listened carefully to what I had to say, and promised to read the gospel literature I left with them. The weather in Melbourne was delightful, but I was told it would be even nicer in Brisbane where my next meetings were to be, in the Conference Hall assembly. It did not turn out that way. Almost every day it rained, not at all cold, indeed very humid but wet. The interest and blessing in the meetings more than made up for the weather. We had the united, hearty fellowship of the assembly. The saints were able to get their friends and neighbours to attend and some got saved. One day, standing at the post office waiting to be attended to, I spoke to another who was waiting. A man standing nearby, hearing my Irish accent came over and I found out that we had been to the same school in Banbridge. After some very friendly conversation, he promised to come to the meetings, which he did, and seemed favourable to the gospel message. I had a short visit to the assembly at Cooroy and was very sorry I did not have a longer time with them, it seemed such a good company. Then I flew to Adelaide for another gospel series. The assembly I was with was very small, but with real exercise in the gospel and for the truth of the assembly. The meetings were not large, but several folk came, and some showed a measure of interest. After that I was in Bexley assembly in Sydney. I stayed with Dr R Wilson and his wife, who is a daughter of the late Mr W Bunting. Some years earlier I had united them in marriage. The meetings were well attended and we had good support from other assemblies. It pleased God to make His presence known and give help. Some were saved and after the meetings, another who was concerned at the meetings got saved.

On my way home I had some meetings in Perth. Mr T Ball was kind, and showed me around the lovely city. I had dinner with him and his wife, and just days later she was suddenly called home. I stayed with a nice Chinese couple I had met in Malaysia, who had moved to Australia. At one of the ministry meetings a doctor's wife said to me, "I would like to speak to you after the meeting", which she did, and told me the following. She said, "When I was a late teenager, on holiday in Ireland, I got saved at your open air meeting in Newcastle". She and her husband were happy and active in the assembly. "Thou shalt find it after many days" (Ecc 11:1). As soon as I got home I told Mr McEwen who had been in the open air meetings. He was now old and frail, but it greatly cheered him. An Irish couple at whose wedding I had officiated had gone to live at Kalgoorlie where the large gold mines are. When they heard I was to be in Perth, they rang me in Sydney and said I must pay them a visit. They arranged for me to fly up from Perth, which I did, and tried to help the small assembly. Generally speaking the men who work in the mines are not interested in divine things, but some came. I was happy to tell them there was "something more than gold".

A couple came to the meetings who work with a mission amongst the Maoris. It was most interesting when I discovered I had met their families whilst having meetings in Devon. Their families were associated with the assemblies there.

The Newtownbreda assembly was interested in one of the large estates in their district and arranged for a large tent to be erected and asked Mr J Allen and me to be responsible for the preaching of the gospel. It turned out to be a very wet season and the site for the tent, that looked so good, turned out to be not so good, and we had a lot of trouble, trying to use plastic sheetings etc to make it as comfortable as possible for the folk. Despite the adverse weather conditions, nice numbers came and God gave help and some got saved. Some of them are now in assembly fellowship.

A further few weeks were spent in conference meetings at Sunderland, Swindon, and ministry meetings in Glenburn, Ballywalter and Carncullagh. The Cookstown assembly asked Mr Aiken and me for a further gospel effort. Both of us had earlier seen blessing there. This time it was different, we could see no interest and did not stay long.

A businessman in Rathfriland, Mr W Toal, was interested in the people of the town. The assemblies in Gransha and Drumlough are both some miles from the town, not really within reach of the townsfolk. Our brother had a large store behind his shop, which had a large concrete yard, good for parking. He cleaned the store and made it very comfortable. Mr Aiken and I started the meetings. It was a real joy to visit the town and country. When Christians have a good testimony, which was true then, it is not difficult to visit and get people to attend. We had lots of town and country people at the meetings. God granted a real sense of His presence and help. Several professed salvation and others showed interest in divine matters. Our brother, his wife and son, along with assembly folk who showed an interest were well rewarded for all the work and expense.

The assembly at Frances Street, Newtownards, asked me if I would join Mr D Gray in gospel meetings. Mr Gray had gone to live in Canada with his uncle Jack, who was well known as an evangelist there. David has been commended to the work of the Lord in Canada. Coming home for a visit to see his mother he was interested to try gospel meetings where, as a boy, he had gone to Sunday School. We had a nice fruitful spell. The attendance was beyond our expectations, very many of the local people came as well as Christians from other assemblies. I enjoyed the meetings with our brother — a simple forthright gospel preacher. He has since been ill and unable to continue in full-time preaching. Some may not realise it, but to preach nightly and visit one needs to be well. The gospel preacher's work is not just an hour in the evening. God gave us to see some blessing in salvation and cheer to the assembly, which of recent years has grown quite a bit.

Due to the troubled conditions of the province, coupled with 'urban decay', many of the city assemblies have been greatly depleted in numbers and strength. Donegall Road is one of these. Once it was a strong and virile company that sent some good men to the mission field, where they were mightily used of God. Mr Aiken and I felt we would like to try and help them. They were glad to know this and encouraged us to try a spell in the gospel. Along with some of the local Christians we visted the whole district daily. We had interesting conversations with many and encouraged them to come to the meetings. We had fairly good numbers and one man professed to be saved. The assembly was encouraged.

I was in ministry for the next month at Letterkenny, Lisburn, Portrush and Gransha. After this, we were in Ballymoney for gospel meetings. Here again God was gracious and gave an excellent interest. Numbers were very good and God's presence a reality. A number professed salvation. It was such a change to be away from sectarian and political strife, a large country town where conditions were peaceable and pleasant.

Ardmore, near the Lough Neagh shore, was the next place of meetings, where I was joined by Mr S Thompson. In earlier years I had fruitful meetings there with Mr McKelvey. Some who had shown an interest then were upon my heart, but sadly I found that whatever interest they had, seemed to have disappeared. We enjoyed visiting the district and giving out tracts, but had to move, seeing no blessing.

Mr Aiken and I went to Omagh, where we had been several times before. Some of these folk are very gracious, they have us again, and yet again! This further spell was blessed of God. The hall was filled nightly. Some nights, the large ante-room was used. While other leaders have been taken away it is nice to see how God has raised up other, younger men to accept responsibility and carry on the way the assembly has done for years. The gospel meetings were blessed and fruitful, a nice number professing salvation.

Kingsbridge is another assembly in Belfast that has grown small and weak. I remember having meetings there when numbers were good. Mr Aiken and I felt we would like to try and help them if we could. I know things are small and the work difficult. It seems a pity though to see the gospel work to an extent neglected. Some get discouraged and give up. We tried a month's meetings and felt it well worthwhile. We didn't have crowds, but we did see good numbers of folk in. The meetings were over for some time before we heard news of salvation —we may yet hear of others. We were not sent to save the people, we were sent to preach the gospel to them and leave God to work.

After this I was joined in Cardy by Mr R Eadie. I had in mind some who regularly attended there, but were not saved. Mr Eadie was interested in other families. The meetings were well attended in a district where numbers are generally not large. God answered prayer and some got saved, who have since been baptised and added to the assembly, but we had to leave others that we had hoped to see gathered in.

Mr Aiken and I went to Killykergan, Co Londonderry, where we spent six and a half weeks, and really enjoyed the time. We had good numbers and interest. One Lord's Day the hall was packed to overflowing, most other nights, well filled. The small surrounding assemblies rallied around us and brought their unsaved families as well as neighbours. God came in and gave us blessing in salvation. The assembly keeps active in the gospel indoors and out of doors. An open-air meeting has been carried on for many years in the town of Garvagh, every Saturday evening.

Glengormley had asked for a week of ministry meetings which were well attended, and in a special way I enjoyed them. The saints asked if we would go for gospel meetings, but since I had promised Mullafernaghan, they said, "Well, we will wait until you finish there, then come to us". Both Mr Aiken and I had been to Mullafernaghan earlier, he with Mr Flanigan, and I with Mr McKelvey and Mr Allen. It is one of those places where from time to time God seems to visit in a real way. 1993 was one of those times. When we arrived it was evident there was a real sense of concern and expectancy. The meetings were not long going until it became evident that God was working. The hall was full each night, people listened attentively. After one or two professed, as I prayed, the words came to me, "Thou shalt see greater things than these". Some long prayed for, and in a sense almost despaired of, professed salvation. While in the goodness of God I have seen blessing, apart from the large series in Toronto, when almost 50 professed, this season was the greatest in Ireland. Asked later at the Easter Conference in Belfast to give a report, I said it would be well to keep in mind that there were times when the Lord Jesus preached and some got saved, and other times some professed and did not go on. It would teach us to speak carefully of our own work and be wise in our comments regarding others. The harvest is the end of the age, not the end of the meetings.

As soon as we finished in Mullafernaghan we went to Glengormley to fulfil the arrangement we had made. After fruitful meetings we almost fear starting afresh. An aged servant of the Lord, Mr G Gould (Sen), said the Lord could not trust him with two good meetings, the one after the other. All our hearts are deceitful and it is so easy to think "we can do it". Sometimes dear brethren fail here, they think if a preacher gets good meetings in one place, "We will invite him". It seldom works. In a way we are happy we had arranged Glengormley before the time of blessing in Mullafernaghan. The Lord was gracious to us again and blessed the meetings where the good and large prayer meetings were a feature at that time. For the nightly meeting the hall was full with God's presence and help being experienced and quite a number professed salvation. One aged overseer said to me at the close of the meetings, "Eight of my grandchildren have been gathered in". They were mostly teenagers. This brought us up to the holiday season.

I have happy memories of Limavady. We went there in early September and spent eight weeks in gospel meetings. When in business in Londonderry I frequently spoke at the Lord's Day evening meeting, and also had an earlier series of tent meetings with Mr F Bingham. In recent times God has blessed in the gospel there, and in His goodness we shared in this in our meetings. A school teacher who had travelled hundreds of miles for years to attend gospel meetings got saved. What seemed to be of help to him was, when he thought of Christ who had borne his sins, now in Heaven. He realised, no sin in Heaven, it must all be put away. God is satisfied and so was he. A Roman Catholic lady got saved, and since conversion, what a transformation. They are both now in assembly fellowship.

A missionary couple, home on furlough from Brazil, had an unsaved daughter studying in Coleraine. The couple arranged to be in the area with a view to getting their girl to the meetings. One night during the course of the meeting the girl broke down and sobbed aloud. The night following she told us of her salvation. She too has gone on well and gives joy in assembly fellowship.

We had an effort in Central Hall, Bangor, a place of earlier very fruitful meetings. This time it was different. We could see no sign of interest and our meetings did not continue long. I have always taken the view, if meetings are good and God is working, then stay, but don't be tied to a diary if there is no interest. Why prolong meetings and weary the saints?

The assembly at Cambridge Avenue, Ballymena, requested

yet another visit. It was Mr Aiken's first time to be with them in special meetings, although this was not the case for me. We found the same interest and co-operation as on other visits. The attendance of local people was quite good and the Lord gave help. Several professed conversion and all have been baptised and received into assembly fellowship, some taking part in a very acceptable way. The Ballymena assemblies take a real interest in the residents of the various residential homes and we were asked to speak at several of the meetings there. It is a joy to see these senior citizens so cared for and cheered with the hymns and messages.

We tried Annalong again and had very good numbers, several showed interest, but only one we know of got saved. It seems so strange, in later times, to see one or two getting saved as in earlier years it was usually a number.

Some in the Wallace Avenue assembly, Lisburn, had an interest in a part of the town (on it's outskirts) and they got a site and borrowed Mr T McNeill's portable hall. Tom is kind and helpful in many ways. It was nice to see quite a number coming who were not accustomed to attending gospel meetings. We enjoyed the presence of the Lord and the hearty co-operation of the Lisburn assemblies and others. No one professed that we know of, but the seed was sown from door to door and from the platform.

After the holiday season we commenced in Broughshane where we had a happy fruitful time. Three professed in the first week and several others as the weeks went on. We got a fair number of people from the village and district where for some years Mr Aiken has had two weeks of open air meetings and tract distribution, so many knew him and came to the hall. We then went to Ballymagarrick, an assembly that has seen the hand of the Lord over the years and many have been saved. Here they carry on an excellent weekly meeting for the children as well, of course, as the Sunday school and Lord's Day evening gospel meetings. We got excellent numbers and night after night the Lord granted His presence and gave much help to preach. In spite of this we had to close and leave without knowing of any getting saved, although one girl got saved after the meetings finished.

In early January 1995 we commenced in Ballintoy, on the

beautiful Antrim coast, where the assembly has prospered in later years. They have built a very commodious hall which Mr Aiken and I had the joy of opening with a gospel meeting. The place was packed. All sorts of folk came, among them local people associated with all kinds of organisations.

We thought when we went for special meetings they would come again, but many didn't. Nevertheless our meetings were encouraging. One lady home on a visit from Australia got saved the morning she left to return home. She has since been contacted and seems to go on well despite not the easiest of circumstances.

After this we were in Enniskillen, where the assembly has grown and goes on nicely. When I had meetings there in the tent in 1950 with Mr S Lewis, the assembly was very weak and struggling. We had good attendance and saw one boy saved. A brother in the assembly responsible for a large cattle mart said many in the place were talking and wondering about the next millennium, and he wondered if he arranged a lunch in his mart, and invited business folk and staff etc, would I give them a message about the 1000 year reign of Christ. I agreed and we had a most happy time. While dealing with the subject I tried to incorporate some gospel truth. When asked to do this, my mind went back to the Bible Class in the assembly at Londonderry. Mr McNee taught the class. There was a young man who was often there. He was slightly weak in his mind, but interested and possibly saved. After Mr McNee spoke one day about the 1000 year reign of Christ, there was time left for questions and comments. The young man said, "Mr McNee, if it rains for 1000 years there will be awful floods?"

We returned to Broughshane and with some ministry tried to help, especially those lately saved.

The assemblies in Cork have carried on a yearly conference on St Patrick's Day, 17th March. I have often been with them and enjoyed the ministry and fellowship. 1995 was their 50th year and they decided to have a special weekend. They invited Dr A J Higgins (USA), Mr J Burnett (Scotland) and Mr D Gilliland (Lurgan) and myself to be the speakers and Mr N McMeekin to look after the children's work. Over 250 were present and a most profitable season it was. In ways the conference there is different. They get a lot of saved people, not all associated with assemblies, and it's a joy to try and help such. The assembly itself is small and weak and needs much help. They meet in the hall in Father Matthew Street, formerly Queen's Street.

A friend of mine went with his wife to Cork City for the weekend. He had learned from another brother of the assembly but had forgotten the name of the street. Not being able to locate the hall he enquired of a taxi driver where the gospel hall was? "Gospel Hall?" said the man, "I've never heard of it." "Well," said my friend, "People called brethren meet in it." "Brethren?" said the man, "I've never heard of them." When my friend insisted the hall and people were there, the man said, "I have driven a taxi in this city for 20 years and I've never heard of it. It's a question if the Man above knows anything about it!"

I went for a week to Kingsmills, where it was a joy to see some present who were saved when we had meetings in the district in 1946, happy in the assembly and seeking to be a help. The folowing week I was in Cardy for ministry.

Mr Aiken and I were invited to Waringstown for gospel meetings in the assembly hall where we enjoyed the visit and had nice numbers to hear the gospel, but little evidence of God working.

Later that winter I joined Mr Cecil and Mr John Rogers in some weeks of gospel meetings in Newry. I was very happy working with these good young men who have the confidence of their own assembly and whose testimony in the district is good. While the meetings were enjoyable and plenty of unsaved were present each night we didn't hear of anyone getting saved.

I was to be with Mr Aiken in Dromore commencing early January 1996, but on Christmas Eve I took ill and for a number of weeks was unable to take part in meetings. I had surgery for prostate gland. This coupled with my diabetic condition left me in poor shape, but with rest and care in the mercy of God, I have been restored to health and back to normal activity. Recovering as I did I had two weeks of gospel meetings in the Lessans, helped by Mr S Thompson. The assembly there has been through very difficult times. Viewing a number of assemblies I cannot but feel they have been the target of satanic attacks. What a mercy if we could all see this and not be ignorant of his devices. As previously mentioned, I have a special interest in the Lessans. My mother as a young woman was in fellowship there and from there in 1917 my father was commended to the work of the Lord. As a small boy staying with my grandmother, I attended meetings there conducted by the evangelist Mr Edward Hughes. I would like to have been saved then. I still have family relations there that I esteem very highly. It was one of these, a man of sixty, that I was particularly interested in with a view to his salvation. The meetings were very well attended, the hall was packed each night, and quite a number of the local people came in. God answered prayer and the man in question got saved, to the joy of all of us and especially to his aged father who has been in the Lessans assembly for 76 years. After some weeks, we tried another two-week spell and again the people came really well and a nice young woman got saved.

The saints in the Strabane assembly were exercised about meetings in their district and knowing how small in numbers they were and yet their concern to reach out in the gospel, Mr Aiken and I felt we would go and try to give what help we could. The village of Artigarvan is a growing area a few miles from Strabane. An elderly sister in Londonderry assembly who was brought up in this village told us the last assembly meetings there were at least 70 years ago, when Mr S Wright and another whose name she could not remember had tent meetings. So it was time to try again! A good site was procured for a portable hall and we started. Not only did we visit daily, but some of the saints who were free did the same. The whole area for several miles was covered and the reception was favourable. In the five weeks we had 25-30 local people in and God blessed in saving a man, who had been long prayed for. Some others showed interest. We may yet hear of further blessing.

The Harryville assembly in Ballymena had invited us for meetings which we had for six weeks. The prayer meetings were most encouraging, with good numbers and a real spirit of exercise among the Christians. On the first Monday night a middle-aged man whose parents have been in the assembly for many years got saved; the Christians were thrilled, as he was brought up in the Sunday School and regularly attended. We had hoped that others connected to him who were also good attenders would get saved, but we had to leave without hearing of their blessing. He has since been baptised and received into assembly fellowship, giving joy and taking a little part. The Harryville meetings took us to almost Christmas.

The following Lord's Day I was at Holywood assembly which has become very small and weak. They were able to have a meeting, only for children, but very few were there.

Fortwilliam have a gospel meeting on the last night of the year. It was good to see the hall full and be able to give a simple gospel message to so many of the neighbours. On the 4th January, Cambridge Avenue assembly, Ballymena, arranged a thanksgiving meeting to celebrate 50 years that Mr R Neill had spent in Africa at which I, with others, was asked to speak. We had an excellent number and a sense of God's presence. It was nice to see our dear brother's work acknowledged.

Laganvale assembly asked me for a further report of my 50 years in the work. Once a month they arrange a late Sunday evening meeting and invite various speakers for missionary reports and other interesting topics. I was cheered to see so many and especially young people. I would pray that God would stir their hearts and they would be able to do something worthwhile with their lives.

I have been happy over the years to have meetings in Bangor. There are four assemblies in that fast-growing seaside town, and I have been privileged to have meetings in all four. Ebenezer was where Mr Aiken and I were in the beginning of 1997. We had eight weeks of well attended meetings and enjoyed the warm-hearted fellowship of the believers. God gave us to see some professing to be saved. Others, who were interested, got saved in later meetings at Ballywalter.

Outside the village of Seapatrick, 73 years ago, after fruitful tent meetings conducted by Mr J McMullan and himself, my father had a small hall erected at Kilpike for children's work. Since then, a Sunday school has been carried on by the believers from the Banbridge assembly. The hall was badly run down and the Banbridge folk had it refurbished, and it was decided to have a short series of gospel meetings in it. Because my father was responsible for the hall being there, they asked if I would have the meetings. The interest was far beyond what we would have expected and the hall was packed each night for two weeks. God gave help and one nice young man in his early twenties got saved. We have since heard of another man who was saved at that time.

Enjoying our 50th Wedding Anniversary.

After the Easter conference meetings Mr Aiken and I commenced in Ballywalter. The Ards peninsula has been a strange, complicated area as far as assembly work has been concerned. We were very happy on this visit to see an improvement in relations and we had much support from neighbouring assemblies. The local interest was encouraging, and God gave us not only large meetings but He moved in our midst in salvation. One who professed was able to tell us he had been several times at the effort in Bangor, and said the second night he was there he discovered he was not right with God. He had no background of gospel teaching, did not have a Bible and was a complete stranger to the things of God. Some who were restored at the meetings have requested baptism and assembly fellowship.

When I had completed 50 years full time service the assembly at Cambridge Avenue, Ballymena, arranged a thanksgiving meeting. It was thought that a good number would attend, but the number was far beyond our expectation. The large hall and ante-rooms were packed and quite a number were turned away, unable to gain admission.

Mr J Wallace was chairman and Mr Mullan, Mr Milne, Mr McFeeters and Mr Neill opened in prayer. Mr McShane, Mr Aiken and Mr Allen gave ministry. I spoke a word of thanks and appreciation and gave a brief report.

I said after the meeting, "I never thought I had so many friends, nor did I think I was such a good boy until I heard my brethren speak." It was a most encouraging meeting. I trust God was glorified and His people blessed.

Soul Winning

In Holy Scripture the features of a wise person are clearly set out. In Proverbs 11:30 it is seen as **soul winning**. It is not preaching, excitement, emotion or counting numbers. We will see there are **reasons** for it.

1. God desires it. He is spoken of as a Saviour God, who will have all men to be saved (1 Timothy 2:4). To make it possible He sent His Son, "Not to condemn the world but that the world through Him might be saved."

2. The Lord Jesus asked His disciples to engage in it, (Mark 1:16-17) "Come and I will make you fishers of men", (Mark 16:15-16) "Preach the gospel to every creature".

3. A sense of duty, seeing the condition of men, blind, helpless and weary, seeing also their position going down and in eternal danger. The Lord Jesus seeing this was "moved with compassion". Paul said, "My heart's desire and prayer" (Romans 10:1). Mr R McCheyne said, "The thud of Christless feet on the way to Hell almost breaks my heart". "Can we to men benighted, the lamp of life deny?"

If there are reasons for it there are also **requirements**:

1. A personal knowledge of salvation. Paul in seeking to win Agrippa relates his conversion experience. The man of Gadara was told to go and tell of his deliverence. It is essential for preacher or counsellor to have a clear definite experience of being saved.

2. A measure of spirituality. A person may have knowledge and ability, but without spirituality it is of no avail. Soul winning is a spiritual work and the workers must be spiritual.

3. There must be sincerity. Insincerity or duplicity have no place in this. Sincerity to please God, to see Christ glorified, to do God's will and to see others blessed. Not a seeking of place, profit or popularity.

4. Consistent conduct. The disciples called to be fishers of men were careful and clean men. They were washing and mending nets. How often we have heard folk say, "it was the way that person lived that spoke to me". The unsaved husband would be won by the chaste conversation of the wife (1Peter 3:1-2).

5. Wisdom. See the wise and careful way the servant in Genesis 24 acted, so handling his master's goods that he won the heart of the young woman and she said, "I will go." Apparently he said nothing critical of her place and company; he showed her something better. So, like Paul, we preach Christ. The soul winner will need to know the Word of God and use it. It is "able to make one wise unto salvation". Leave all other modern ideas and preach Christ.

There are **rewards** for this noble service:

1 The joy of doing God's will. Many a lonely labourer plods on, assured that while men may not applaud, he is in the will of God.

2. The joy of seeing others blessed. The shepherd in Luke 15 said, "Rejoice with me I have found the sheep that was lost." What joy the salvation of a soul brings to the winner.

3. The pleasure of adding to Heaven's joy, Luke 15:7. What an amazing truth that by soul winning we cause joy in Heaven; better doing that than causing grief and sorrow here.

4. A reward awaits the worker, John 4:36; 1 Thessalonians 2:19. Paul looked forward to seeing his converts in glory. Mr Rutherford said, "If one soul from Anworth meets me at God's right hand, my heaven will be two heavens in Immanuel's land."

A brother in Iowa, USA, who while he farmed spent very much of his time preaching the gospel, was asked what he thought about the lost tribes of Israel. He said he was more concerned about the lost souls in Iowa. May God stir our hearts and help us sing with reality:

O come let us go and find them,
In the paths of death they roam,
At the close of the day, 'twill be sweet to say.
I have brought some lost one home.

Preachers

It has been my privilege to know and company with a number of full-time workers. I have found these dear men helpful and kind, and have learned a great deal by listening to them and observing them.

All the full-time workers who were in Northern Ireland when I started out have passed away, save two, Mr McShane, a few years my senior and still active in gospel preaching and teaching, and Mr H Paisley who has lived for many years in Canada and laboured seeing God's hand in blessing.

It is only to be expected that in such a company of men, there would, at times, be a different approach to some matters. Thinking of one's attitude and conduct to fellow workers it is well to keep in mind what the Lord said to Saul of Tarsus on the Damascus Road, "Why persecutest thou Me?" When we injure another believer, we hurt Christ. When Paul withstood Peter, Galatians 2:11, it was "to his face", not a whispering behind his back, and it was because he loved him and sought his welfare. Some of these early labourers were characters, most original, and it is for this reason I mention some of the things they said and did.

Mr J K McEwen came originally from the Dromore area where he was saved. He was mightly used of God in many places, especially Nova Scotia. He was the first assembly worker to go there. In some parts of that land, the Christians are still called "McEwenites". He was a sharp penetrative preacher who was not moved by either the favour or frown of men. At a conference in Donemana in County Tyrone, Dr Matthews, who more or less assumed leadership at these meetings, called on Mr McEwen to pray, saying, "We will wait on you". There was no response and the doctor repeated his call. Still there was no response at which the doctor started to pray saying, "O Lord we wait on Thee," to which Mr McEwen interjected, "That is much better".

At a conference in New England, USA, on a warm sultry

A group of "Chief men among the brethren" Easter Conference 1947.

Lord's Day afternoon, a missionary was giving a report and at a point spoke of a time when he was at the end of his resources. Just than a letter arrived from a widow with exactly the money he needed. At this, Mr McEwen shouted out, "What is her name and address?" It had an electrifying effect on the whole conference. Writing to an assembly he had seen formed in Wales he expressed a desire to visit them. They would have been happy to have him but their funds were low. In a veiled way they replied asking if he would postpone his visit to which he replied, "I will be with you on such and such a day arriving by train, enclosed please find two pounds for expenses."

He was not happy about circular letters from workers. When he would hear one read, he would whisper to one beside him, "Grandma". The background was that a small boy wanted a bicycle and was told that if he prayed for it he might get it. He started to pray at the top of his voice. Some said, "You don't need to shout, God isn't deaf". "I know that", said the boy "but Grandma is". While Mr McEwen would have spoken clearly about money, it was not that he sought it, rather, he was a generous giver. A young evangelist pioneering in a southern state of the USA, one day received a little brown envelope with an English post mark. It was from Mr McEwen with just the amount of money the young man needed to pay his lodgings.

Mr Gilmore was saved as a youth in Co Down and went out preaching when very young. He used to say when very old, "They said when I started I was too young, now they say I am too old". He had a desire to live to 100, but only reached 95. When I got married he said to me, "I didn't think I would live to be 30, and I thought it was not worthwhile, I am sorry I did not" — let bachelors take note. He lived for many years in Bangor where a kind friend supplied him with an annual first class ticket for Belfast. One day a critical person saw him get into a first class carriage and said, "Is this the way you look after the Lord's money?" "No," he said, "This is the way I look after the Lord's servant." A young man was asked to open a meeting for him and in doing so, he took up almost the whole of his time. As he finished he said, "Mr Gilmore will now give us his address". Quietly, Mr Gilmore said, "My address is Gray's Hill, Bangor, shall we close in prayer."

Lurgan: Mr McShane 50 years preaching, 1994.
Left to right, Back Row: G Stewart; N Stewart; D Gilliland; N Turkington; S McBride; N Wilson.
Front Row: J G Hutchinson; S Ferguson ; E Fairfield; A McShane; T Bentley.

After a conference another speaker said to him, "I heard you give that address, almost word for word at a conference." "Did you" he asked "did you speak?" "I did" replied the other. "Well" said Mr Gilmore, "I don't remember a word you said".

At a large conference in Glasgow where he was a regular visitor a speaker was saying, "The day has come when we need an educated ministry, learned men". Mr Gilmore followed him reading 1 Chronicles 12:18. He began to speak saying, "I totally disagree with the former speaker. It is not learned men we need, it is loyal men we need". At the close of the conference the chairman thanking the speakers said, "You will all agree the Irish man is the hardest hitter we have, but we are inviting him back next year". He was approached by two wealthy business-men who had a care for him. They asked had he made provision for the days when he would not be able to travel and preach. "Yes," he said, "I have. The God who called me and has supported me all my long life will care for me." No doubt the dear men had in mind suggesting to help him, but his trust was in God.

Mr R Love was of farming stock and retained that appearance all his life. He was saved in Co Armagh. He spent his very long life in gospel work, much of it in the Irish Republic. Speaking to believers about their position and being in the assembly he would say, "Some tell us you should stay where you got the blessing". That is, if you were saved in a church or mission hall you should stay there. He would say, "If I stayed where I got the blessing I would be standing in a grazing field".

During a period of controversy regarding the coming of the Lord. A number of responsible brethren were standing talking after a Bible reading, Mr Love amongst them. A well taught speaker came over and said, "Mr Love, could you tell us what you think about this?" "Yes," he said, "stand there and I will tell you", so having done that he said to the brother, "What do you think of that?" The brother replied, "I would not be sure," "Well," said Mr Love, "I could tell you God's truth but I cannot put brains into you". They parted on good terms as both had a sense of humor.

Mr F Knox came from Co Monaghan and was saved after attending meetings in a large tent in Belfast, conducted by Mr A

Brethren responsible for revising the Gospel Hymn Book.
Left to right: A Badger; J Strahan; J Wallace; J G Hutchinson; J Lennox.
(Mr J Hawthorne due to illness not in picture) At Mr Wallace's home.

Jardine and Mr D Rea. Mr Knox was a forthright, plain preacher who had no time for anything light or foolish. He was a diligent visitor in homes, hospitals and jails. He was a wise visitor knowing that when people are ill, long visits and wearying prayers are not good, so he would read a verse or two and pray. While some may not have liked his plain preaching, all were agreed that when he prayed you felt he was in touch with God. Likely his greatest work was in the city of Belfast with the big tent. In it many were saved. When he was very old and more or less feeble, a friend took him for a short drive and stopped at the Castlereagh hills where they viewed the city.

Mr Knox said, "Belfast, I am free from your blood".

There was hardly a street or house where he had not visited or left gospel tracts.

I was having meetings in Lurgan when his daughter rang me to say her father was in hospital and would I go to see him. I was due home the next night and thought I would see him then. On second thoughts, I went at once and am glad I did. He was very ill, and I asked him if he would like me to read, so I read Psalm 23. As soon as I finished he said, "The greatest word is *forever* ". Eternal things were very real to him whether he preached or prayed. That night he was called home.

Mr John Moneypenny, a veteran preacher, came from the Dungannon area and went with his family to Canada where some of them prospered in business. He got saved when he was 19 and from the very first was deeply interested in divine matters. He was a true pioneer in Canada and the USA, as well as working in many other places with God's blessing attending his work. Soon after his homecall, Mr Aboud, an evangelist in Egypt, wrote saying, "Mr Moneypenny was a real man of prayer." As a servant of the Lord Jesus Christ our dear brother was very conscientious in the use of his time. From early morning to night he was busy distributing tracts, talking to sinners, taking a meeting, visiting some needy saints. He spent seven years in Egypt where his daughter taught English in Cairo. An esteemed overseer in a large well-to-do assembly said to me after the funeral. "Brother Jim, we feel ashamed and condemned. When the lady who had the Christian guest house where Mr Moneypenny stayed, and in whose home he was found dead upon his knees, sent for us to look after his body, we found he hadn't a pound in the world." It is well the record is on high.

Mr H Bailie was brought up in Belfast and in early life he excelled in playing football. He would often say that even amidst the cheers and applause of the crowd he felt lonely and uneasy knowing he had a sister who was praying for his salvation. After long periods of anxiety and longing for peace, at a point he said, "If I go to Hell I will go trusting Christ". He got saved and matured in divine matters, became a keen student of Holy Scripture and a very acceptable speaker. I recall hearing him one day at a large conference in Bleary. Speaking of the resurrection of Christ he said, "I know He is alive, I was speaking to Him this morning". It was evident from his manner of life and preaching that he knew much of the Lord and communed with Him.

Before Mr Bunting took ill and was called home, he asked me if I would assist him in compiling a book of Irish Evangelists. I was happy to agree and be of help. But before the work commenced Mr Bunting took ill and died. I thought I should carry on with the suggestion. In 1969 the book entitled *Irish Evangelists now with the Lord* was published. In 1984 another was published, an update of the former, it was called *Sowers, Reapers, Builders*. In 1988 *Missionaries from Ireland* was published and all were well accepted and soon sold out. In 1993 I was asked by Gospel Tract Publications to compile a book regarding Mr Frank Knox, a worthy and much used servant of God [On going to press this book is still available].

When the Gospel Hymn Book, which had been in circulation for many years, and had been a blessing, was going out of print it was thought advisable to do some revision before reprinting. Mr J S Wallace, Mr J Lennox, Mr J Hawthorne, Mr J Strahan, Mr A Badger and myself were asked if we would undertake the task of revision. A number of hymns were left out and a number of others were included. The earlier edition had 712 hymns, the new one has 795. There was a fair amount of time and work put into it, renumbering, arrangements of hymns and a completely new index, and on the whole, the new book is well received and being used in a number of assemblies. Others will wait until their present stock is worn out. In response to many requests, a music edition has been produced which will be nice for the Christian home and no doubt useful to the brethren who lead the singing. We were very sorry that Mr Hawthorne did not live to see the book published, after he had put so much work and interest into it, but he is now singing in Heaven's choirs.

When I left business, I had no idea of the problems that existed between assemblies and evangelists. My father, though he knew of them, never talked about them in our presence. I have tried in some measure to follow the good example, not to repeat and talk all over the country about what I hear and know. God has said, "Thou shalt not go up and down as a talebearer among thy people" (Leviticus 19:16, see also Proverbs 26:20). Only in one home have I seen this text framed and displayed. Good if it was in many more!

A Scottish evangelist for whom I had great regard was visiting in a Christian's home one evening. In the course of the evening, the conversation turned to men who preach, and some critical things were said. My friend stood up and said , "I was brought up in a home where the servants of God were esteemed and loved and I am not happy to participate in this conversation".

Another thing I never heard my father speak of was money matters. In 45 years of full-time preaching, no doubt he had trying times. He died in hospital after surgery, and my mother told me that when he went into hospital, he had £18 in the world. Let those who criticise preachers take note. Appearances can be deceiving. He would have given away nearly all he received to help others. I said when I went out preaching that only God and my wife will know whether I have money or not. I don't even discuss it with fellow preachers.

Conclusion

As I bring this book to a close, I would like first of all to record my thanks to God for His faithfulness and care, guiding and helping me, preserving me in travel, testimony and health. At

Our family.

times when I had many shortcomings and failures and my mind would wander and my heart grow cold, God would restore me and inspire me to greater devotion and more diligent service. Young Christian, you can with confidence and joy live for and serve such a God. "Not one good thing hath failed" (Joshua 23:15).

After moving among the Lord's people for all these years I would like to pay tribute to them, for the way they have supported and encouraged me. Only God knows how often they have gone to great lengths to be of help. While many who showed an interest in me have been called home, many others have been raised up to take their place in helping in the furtherance of the work of God.

Looking back I feel had I stayed in business, in all likelihood I would have prospered and perhaps been successful in accumulating money and possessions, but God had said, "A man's life consisteth not in the abundance of the things which he possesseth". A little while ago I was at the funeral of a well-to-do Christian, a good man who had built a fine home. As the coffin was being carried out of the house, this verse came in freshness to my mind. I feel like godly Rutherford who said, "If one soul from Anworth meet me at God's right hand, my heaven will be two heavens in Emmanuel's land".

I feel I would like, if I could, to stir the hearts of young believers "to set your affection on things above" (Colossians 3:1-2), not meaning they should give up secular employment and be either evangelists or missionaries, but they should "seek first the kingdom of God" (Matthew 6:33).

INDEX OF PHOTOGRAPHS

Index of Photographs